MISTY RICARDO'S CURRY

INDIAN RESTAURANT
CURRY AT HOME
VOLUME 2

RICHARD SAYCE

Copyright © 2019 Richard Sayce

First published in 2019 by Misty Ricardo's Curry Kitchen

All rights reserved.

No part of this publication may be reproduced, stored in a retrieval system, or transmitted, in any form or by any means, electronic, mechanical, photocopying, recording or otherwise, without prior written permission of the author.

Although the author has made every effort to ensure that the information in this book was correct at press time, the author and publisher do not assume and hereby disclaim any liability to any party for any loss, damage, or disruption caused by errors or omissions, whether such errors or omissions result from negligence, accident, or any other cause.

ISBN: 978-1-9996608-1-9

First Printed : March 2019, UK

Book design: Richard Sayce

Editor: Gary Crossley

Cover photo & design: Richard Sayce

All other photos and artwork: Richard Sayce, unless otherwise stated.

All recipes created by the author unless stated otherwise.

All associated YouTube videos filmed and edited by the author.

Additional copies of this paperback and Volume 1 can be ordered worldwide (subject to availability) from www.mistyricardo.com

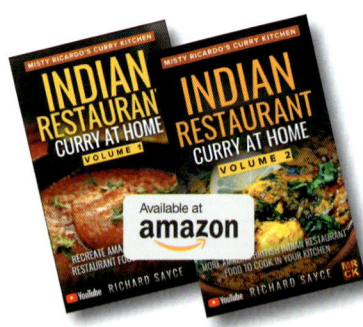

Kindle eBook versions of both Volume 1 and Volume 2 of INDIAN RESTAURANT CURRY AT HOME are available at www.amazon.co.uk and Amazon stores worldwide.

 YouTube   www.youtube.com/MistyRicardo

 Facebook   www.facebook.com/MistyRicardosCurryKitchen

 Instagram   www.instagram.com/mistyricardo/

 Twitter   www.twitter.com/MistyRicardo

Contents

Foreword	4
General Information	6
Getting Started	8
New Mix Powder & Base Gravy	10
Bassar Mix Powder	11
Base Gravy (Mark II)	12
Pre-Prepared Ingredients (from Volume 1)	15
Mix Powder	15
Base Gravy (Mark I)	16
Ginger/Garlic Paste	18
Tomato Paste	18
Pre-Cooked Chicken	19
Pre-Cooked Lamb	20
Chicken Tikka	21
Starters & Sides	23
Prawn Puri	24
Achari Chicken Tikka	26
Malai Chicken Tikka	28
Keema Peas	30
Chicken Pakoras	33
Vegetable Samosa	35
Brinjal Bhaji	37
Mushroom Bhaji	39
Bhindi Fry	41
Restaurant Style Curries	43
Coriander & Lemon Achari Mirch	44
Methi Chicken	46
Achari Lamb	48
King Prawn Zafrani	51
Kalimirch	54
Shimla Mirch	56
Pudina	58
Kashmir	61
Moghul	64
Chicken Tikka Shashlik	66
Adrak	68
Shorshe Masala	70
Lamb Chana Saagwala	73
Shahee Chicken Tikka	75
Mango Chicken	78
Pasanda	80
Mr Naga	82
LavaStorm	84
South Indian Tamarind	88
Special Vegetarian Curries	91
Egg Bhuna	92
Spinach & Mushroom Balti	94
Punjabi Vegetable 'Staff' Curry	97
Chana Masala	100
Saag Paneer	102
Kadai Paneer	105
Rice	109
Lemon Rice	110
Cumin & Onion Pilau	112
Street Food & Other Oddities	113
Chilli & Tomato Chutney	114
Green Chutney	116
Chicken 65	118
Bunny Chow	121
Masala Toast	124
Bassar Fried Chicken	126
Homestyle Lamb Curry	128
Mango Lassi	131
Cheesy Peas	132
Chilli Cheese Toast	134
Upscaling Curry	135
Inside an Indian Restaurant Kitchen	149
Acknowledgements	157
INDEX	158

Foreword

Hello once again and welcome to the second book in my series about making British Indian Restaurant (BIR) style food at home.

In Volume 2 I branch out further into the world of BIR food to bring you many more restaurant-style recipes that I hope you will make and enjoy. Amongst these are new base gravy and mix powder recipes, and some unusual items that range from Indian street food to some rather 'left-field' dishes which may surprise you!

There are also chapters dedicated to popular subjects such as scaling recipes up beyond a single portion, and about working life inside an Indian restaurant kitchen.

This book is a natural progression from my first book, INDIAN RESTAURANT CURRY AT HOME Volume 1, and I hope that it meets with the same approval.

To date (as of late 2018) Volume 1 has flourished in both paperback and Kindle eBook formats, and has, on occasions, topped the Amazon Kindle charts in the Asian Cookbook category. I was also recently informed that it had won an award for the best UK self-published cookbook in the 2019 Gourmand World Cookbook Awards, which was a wonderful and unexpected surprise.

I would like to take this opportunity to thank everyone who bought the book, and for the continual support and contributions by the many who follow Misty Ricardo's Curry Kitchen on Facebook, YouTube, Twitter and Instagram.

It's enormously satisfying as a self-publishing author to see the effort rewarded by the hundreds of photos of MRCK recipes submitted on social media by my readers. I have included several collages throughout this book which show off just a few of those photos. Thank you again to everyone.

I extend to you a warm invitation to get stuck in and get your kitchen messy, but not before reading the introductory chapters, which will give you some important information.

Richard Sayce

Please note that all spoon measurements in this book are LEVEL unless mentioned otherwise.

1 tsp = 5ml

1 TBSP = 15ml

Photo Collage A: Curry Heaven. The curry spread (top middle) by Carl Hodgson is particularly impressive.

General Information

Recipe Conventions & Measurements

- tsp = teaspoon = 5ml
- TBSP = tablespoon = 15ml
- Spoon measurements are level unless stated otherwise.
- Base gravy should be added in a <u>watered-down</u> state when cooking a curry with it. The consistency should be that of semi-skimmed milk, which is approximately twice as thin as my base gravy recipes produce.
- The term '<u>Tomato Paste</u>' when mentioned in this book refers to blended plum tomatoes or to tomato purée diluted with three times the amount of water.
- 'Oil', unless stated otherwise, refers to neutral tasting oils such as sunflower, vegetable, rapeseed, etc.
- 'Ghee', unless stated otherwise, refers to either vegetable or butter ghee.
- One peeled medium-sized onion weighs approximately 150g.

Recipe Portion Sizes

All curry recipes in the book (unless stated otherwise) are for a generous single portion of the same quantity you would expect from an Indian takeaway: plenty enough for one person, or possibly two with smaller appetites.

The amount of the main curry ingredient (chicken, lamb, prawns, vegetables, etc.) is at your discretion. I suggest including between 175-200 grams in each recipe curry portion.

Is Volume 1 Needed?

Those of you who own my previous book, INDIAN RESTAURANT CURRY AT HOME Volume 1, will know that it includes (amongst other things) a comprehensive introduction to BIR (British Indian Restaurant) cooking, a glossary of spices, recipes for all the most common restaurant menu items, and a detailed exploration of how various cooking methods can help you make curries of restaurant quality (or better).

However, it is NOT essential to own or have read Volume 1 to use this book. I've made sure that all the recipes stand alone in their own right, and I've concisely repeated the fundamental recipes for pre-prepared ingredients. These include mix powder, base gravy, ginger/garlic paste, tomato paste, chicken tikka, and recipes for pre-cooking chicken and lamb.

With that having been said, I do recommend you invest in a copy of Volume 1. It contains many excellent recipes, and as I mentioned in an earlier paragraph, it has a very detailed section on cooking technique, which is as crucial a part of cooking BIR food as the ingredients themselves.

On the next page is an image showing the Volume 1 table of contents, which I hope will make your mouth water and cause you to consider forking out.

I'm confident you will be happy to own a copy of Volume 1, which is available worldwide and can be bought in paperback format from www.mistyricardo.com, and in Kindle format at Amazon.

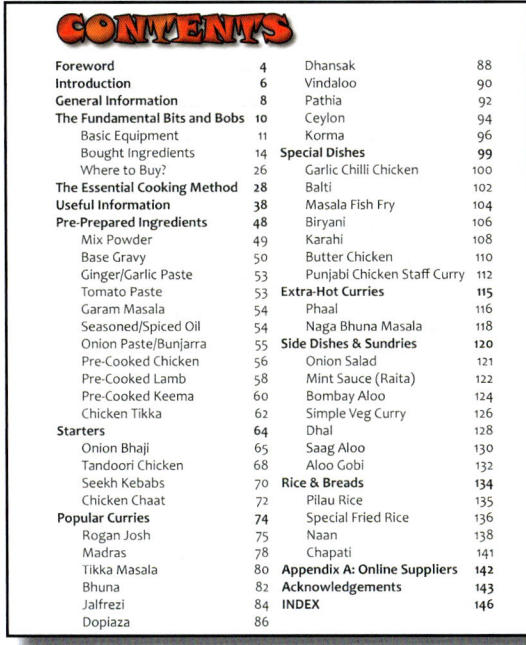

www.mistyricardo.com   Amazon (Kindle eBook)

YouTube Video Channel

There is an accompanying video demonstrating exactly how to make all but a few of this book's recipes. The 'Misty Ricardo's Curry Kitchen' YouTube channel was born several years ago and has grown to include over 100 (mainly recipe) videos.

You will see a QR code to the right of the heading for each recipe that has a corresponding video. Scan with a smartphone or tablet to get direct access to the YouTube video. The recipes match the videos exactly, except for a very few minor tweaks, which I've detailed in the notes where applicable. If in doubt follow the book recipe, but please do watch the videos as they demonstrate the all-important technique in visual detail, as well as being amusing in parts.

Facebook, Instagram & Twitter

Misty Ricardo's Curry Kitchen has an interactive, busy and friendly Facebook page (www.facebook.com/MistyRicardosCurryKitchen). It has thousands of followers, and some of them post pictures of the food they have made by following my recipes. You can also visit Misty Ricardo's Curry Kitchen on Instagram and Twitter.

Below are QR Codes which you can scan with a smartphone or tablet to visit the various social media sites.

YouTube   Facebook   Instagram   Twitter

Getting Started

If you are new to the British Indian Restaurant (BIR) style of cooking, you will find this section informative.

Although BIR style curry usually takes less than 10 minutes to cook, it involves quite a lot of pre-prepared ingredients, and this can be daunting to the newcomer. But no matter how much time and effort is involved, it's worth it!

Everything that needs preparing in advance can be made in large batches and frozen for future use in handy portion sizes. Once that work is out of the way, you won't need to do it again until something needs replenishing.

In the main I'm referring to arguably the most vital curry ingredient – base gravy. This is the lifeblood that you will always want available in case of those sudden curry cravings! My base gravy recipes make enough for about 16 curry recipe portions, and under normal circumstances that's sufficient to keep my household going for several weeks.

I also find it desirable to have batches of frozen pre-cooked chicken, pre-cooked lamb, and chicken tikka prepared. I store them mostly in small freezer bags in 200g amounts, which I subsequently use in single recipe portion curries. Being relatively quick to cook, it's not mandatory to pre-cook raw chicken before making a curry with it, but I recommend that you do so. My pre-cooked chicken recipe produces flavoursome and tender results, and it's worth the extra work.

Most of the ingredients in a curry need no cooking in advance, but it's a good idea to be organised and make them ready and accessible. For example, mix powder, which is a combination of several different spices, should be mixed together in advance.

All your spices (especially powdered ones) will thank you for being kept dark and airtight, so keep them in sealed containers that are quickly accessible when you are cooking. I use small, labelled glass jars with tight lids which hold about 100ml, and keep the most commonly used ones in a convenient kitchen drawer.

It's a similar situation for ginger/garlic paste. Once blended, a batch of it can be emptied into ice cube trays, frozen, and then transferred into airtight freezer bags. Cubes of the paste can then be taken out and defrosted quickly, as and when required. You may opt to buy 100% pure ginger/garlic paste in frozen block form, which is now available in most supermarkets. I find it to be an acceptable and very convenient alternative.

So, for those of you who have yet to take the first steps of your BIR journey, please continue reading for suggestions that will help make your first curry cooking session pain-free – and fun!

1. Prepare some mix powder.
2. Make some ginger/garlic paste (or buy it ready frozen).
3. Cook a batch of base gravy, freezing what you don't intend to use imminently.
4. Choose a relatively simple curry to make from this book (or indeed Volume 1 if you own it). From this book I suggest you opt for mushroom bhaji. Strictly speaking it's a starter (or side-dish), but it's the simplest recipe, and it's still essentially a base gravy-based dish that is cooked like a curry.

5. Make sure you've got all the recipe ingredients to hand before starting to cook. Have enough hot and watered-down base gravy in a saucepan accompanied by a ladle. Make sure your main ingredient has defrosted, ready your tomato paste, and measure out all the other ingredients (ramekin bowls are good for this). Have everything ready and organised for when you start cooking.

6. Follow the recipe exactly. Good luck and keep practising!

More useful information about where to start, where to buy, what equipment to use, and more is in Volume 1 of INDIAN RESTAURANT CURRY AT HOME.

As foundation layers of building a BIR curry, the mix powder and base gravy ingredients are the lifeblood of every dish. They set the theme for every curry you cook using them. It's important to get a good balance of flavours from the start, but without any one ingredient dominating the flavour, otherwise all curries would taste very similar.

My original base gravy and mix powder recipes were included in Volume 1 and are repeated later in this book for your convenience. I would describe them as an excellent 'all-round' foundation that set the stage for mainstream British Indian Restaurant curry cooking. From herein I will refer to the original base gravy as 'Mark I'.

But as all curry lovers know, spice is the variety of life, and it's refreshing to try something alternative. To that end I have created new recipes for base gravy and mix powder. Feel free to 'mix and match'. Read on...

Bassar Mix Powder

Bassar is a curry powder that is frequently used in Pakistani cuisine. It has a high proportion of chilli powder and other pungent spices, which lends itself well to spicy tomato-based curries.

Here is my formula for a bassar mix powder, which can be used instead of the Volume 1 mix powder to give a sharper, hotter flavour for those who like a little creeping heat at the back of the throat. Just 1-1½ tsp of this mix powder will impart a nice, diverse taste and a spicy kick to a BIR curry. One teaspoon of it contains around a quarter to a third a teaspoon of chilli powder, so if you wish you can compensate by reducing the amount of extra chilli powder you add to a curry recipe (if it calls for it).

You can buy bassar curry powder from Asian supermarkets or online. It's usually sold in 100g or 400g bags. Various brands are available - Al Noor, Alamgeer, Heera and King of Spice, amongst many others.

To prepare the mix powder, grind the (untoasted) cumin and coriander seeds finely and mix with the other powdered spices. You can make any amount you wish, of course - just scale up or down making sure the ratios are maintained.

- 3 TBSP Bassar Curry Powder
- 1½ TBSP Turmeric
- 1 TBSP Paprika
- ¾ TBSP Cumin Seeds
- ¾ TBSP Coriander Seeds

Make sure to check out my Bassar Fried Chicken recipe on page 126 to make good use of this version of mix powder.

Base Gravy (Mark II)

Here we have an alternative to the Misty Ricardo Mark I base gravy. This one has a savoury feel to it, as it's more refined and has a touch more of a 'grown up' flavour. It has a little less sweetness due to the omission of carrot and coconut, but adds two new vegetables to the pot: celery and white cabbage. Both of these add a pleasant piquancy and provide a nice contrast to the sweetness of onions.

Cassia bark (or cinnamon powder) is given the chance to play a minor supporting role – an extra that's not especially noticeable except by its absence. Note: don't forget to remove the cassia bark before blending the base.

Key to this base is the use of my new bassar mix powder. One of the components of this new mix is bassar curry powder, a commercially available Pakistani spice blend which has a heavier proportion of pungent spices than mild madras curry powder, not least amongst which is chilli powder.

So, for a refreshing change, consider cooking up a batch of this savoury golden liquid and use it in your curries. The cooking method is identical to the Mark I base gravy (see page 16), but I've repeated it here for convenience.

This recipe will make enough base gravy for about 16 single recipe portion curries.

Stage 1 Ingredients

- 200ml Oil
- 1½kg Brown Onions, peeled and roughly chopped (unpeeled weight). Peeled weight approx. 1¼kg
- ½ Green Pepper, chopped
- 100g Celery, chopped (approximately 2 long sticks)
- 120g White Cabbage, chopped (approximately ¼ of a small-medium sized one)
- 100g Potato, roughly chopped (peeled weight)
- 80g Ginger/Garlic Paste
- 1½ tsp Salt

Stage 2 Ingredients

- 2 TBSP Bassar Mix Powder
- 1 tsp Turmeric
- ½ tsp Garam Masala
- 5cm Cassia Bark or ¼-½ tsp Cinnamon Powder (optional)
- 160g Tomato Purée (double concentrated, good quality)
- 2 Litres Water
- 40g fresh Coriander Stalks, chopped (optional)

Stage 1 Method

1. Add the oil to a large pan (minimum 5 litres capacity) and heat to medium.
2. Add the onions, celery, white cabbage, green pepper, potato, ginger/garlic paste, and salt.
3. Fry for 5 minutes, stirring frequently.
4. Cover and turn down heat to very low to achieve a gentle simmer.
5. Cook for one hour or until the onions soften fully, taking on a melted appearance and releasing a soft, sweet, delicious smell. Stir occasionally.

Stage 2 Method

1. Turn the heat up to medium and add the bassar mix powder, turmeric, and garam masala. Also add the optional cassia bark or cinnamon powder, if using.
2. Cook for 1 minute whilst stirring, then add the tomato purée, and water. Stir well.
3. Bring to the boil, then cover, turn the heat down to low, and gently simmer for 1 hour, stirring very occasionally.
4. Optional: add the coriander stalks a few minutes before the end of the hour.
5. Turn the heat off and allow the gravy to cool a little.
6. Remove the cassia bark (if using).

Stage 3 Method

1. Blend until very smooth. I prefer to use a stick blender.
2. Bring back up to boil, and simmer gently for 20-30 minutes.
3. Turn off the heat and allow to cool. Stir together and blend again if you see any lumps.
4. The base gravy will be quite thick when you have finished making it. It's unlikely you will be using it all at once, so it's best to refrigerate or freeze what you aren't using. I freeze mine in its thickened state in plastic food containers and defrost when needed.

Notes

a) If using cassia bark please remember to retrieve it from the pan before blending, or the base gravy will be overpowered with the taste of cinnamon.
b) The base gravy should be quite <u>thin</u> when cooking a BIR curry. Dilute it with an equal amount of water to get a consistency of semi-skimmed milk, and always heat it up before using it to avoid slowing the curry cooking process and impeding the flavour.
c) You can make smaller or larger amounts of base gravy by simply scaling this recipe down or up.
d) Remember that all spoon measurements are level unless otherwise specified. 1 tsp = 5ml, 1 TBSP = 15ml.

Pressure Cooking Base Gravy

You can shave about an hour from the total cooking time by using a pressure cooker. The process I use is almost identical to making base gravy in a conventional pot.

In Stage 1, once the vegetables have been fried for 5 minutes (step 3), seal the lid onto the pressure cooker and bring to pressure on highest heat. Once pressurised turn the heat to low and leave for about 15 minutes. Then release the pressure and uncover ready for the next stage.

For Stage 2, when you've stirred in the step 2 ingredients, seal the lid again and perform the same actions as Stage 1. If you are adding the coriander stalks do so once the pressure has been released, and simmer for 5 minutes.

Stage 3 remains unchanged.

Photo Collage B: A fine array of 'nomaliciousness'. I particularly like the lamb vindaloo photo (2nd row, 2nd column) by Gillian Watt Divine.

Pre-Prepared Ingredients (from Volume 1)

In this chapter you will find my recipes for making the key components of British Indian Restaurant (BIR) cooking. These recipes are already included in INDIAN RESTAURANT CURRY AT HOME Volume 1, but to make it possible to use this book independently I have replicated them here, albeit in condensed form and without the photographs.

As a bonus I have also replicated my chicken tikka recipe, which is of course used as an ingredient in curries as well as being eaten as a starter or a snack.

Mix Powder

Mix powder is a mixture of basic masalas and spices that is used in most British Indian Restaurants to form the basis of the spicing. This is the recipe I use, which I find gives a good foundation of flavour to curries in conjunction with my base gravy.

This recipe will make enough mix powder for at least 12 single portion curries. The ingredients can be simply scaled up if required.

1 TBSP Cumin Seeds (freshly ground)
1 TBSP Coriander Seeds (freshly ground)
1½ TBSP Turmeric Powder
½ TBSP Paprika (NOT smoked)
1½ TBSP Mild Madras Curry Powder
¼ tsp Garam Masala

Grind the cumin and coriander seeds in a coffee grinder or pestle & mortar. Mix with the other ingredients in a bowl and store in a clean, dry, airtight container, away from heat and light.

Base Gravy (Mark I)

Arguably the most important ingredient, base gravy is an essential part of creating the amazing flavour in British Indian Restaurant style cooking. Setting a theme with its simple ingredients, it is the fundamental backbone to the flavour, and combined with the right cooking techniques helps give a wonderful, caramelised, almost smoky taste.

This recipe was a result of considerable experimentation to find the balance of flavours I wanted. It's a safe, all-round sauce that ticks all the right boxes for BIR cooking, but remember it's not so much what's in it, but what you do with it that counts. See my new base gravy Mark II recipe on page 12 for a more savoury alternative.

This recipe will make enough base gravy for about 16 single portion curries.

Stage 1 Ingredients

- 200ml Oil, 1½kg Brown Onions, peeled and roughly chopped (unpeeled weight). Peeled weight approx. 1¼kg
- 75-100g Carrot, chopped small (approx. half a large one), ½ Green Pepper, chopped (medium large)
- 100g Potato, roughly chopped (peeled weight), 80g Ginger/Garlic Paste, 1½ tsp Salt

Stage 2 Ingredients

- 2 TBSP Mix Powder, 1 tsp Turmeric, 1 tsp Garam Masala
- 160g Tomato Purée (good quality), 40g Coconut Block (or 80ml Coconut Milk)
- 1 tsp Jaggery or Brown Sugar (optional), 2 Litres Water
- 40g fresh Coriander Stalks, chopped (optional)

Stage 1 Method

1. Add the oil to a large pan (minimum 5 litres capacity) and turn heat to medium.
2. Add the onions, carrot, green pepper, potato, ginger/garlic paste, and salt. Cook for 5 minutes, stirring frequently.
3. Cover and turn down heat to very low, to achieve a gentle simmer. Cook for one hour, or until the onions soften fully, taking on a melted appearance and releasing a soft, sweet, delicious smell. Stir occasionally.

Stage 2 Method

1. Turn the heat up to medium and add the mix powder, turmeric and garam masala. Cook for 1 minute whilst stirring. Then add the tomato purée, coconut, jaggery (optional), and water. Stir well.
2. Bring to the boil, then cover, turn the heat down to low, and gently simmer for 1 hour, stirring very occasionally. Optional: add the coriander stalks a few minutes before the end of the hour.
3. Turn heat off and allow the gravy to cool a little.

Stage 3 Method

1. Blend until very smooth. I prefer to use a stick blender.
2. Bring back up to boil, and simmer gently for 20-30 minutes.
3. Turn off the heat and allow to cool. Stir together and blend again if you see any lumps.
4. The base gravy will be quite thick when you have finished making it. It's unlikely you will be using it all at once, so it's best to refrigerate or freeze what you aren't using. I freeze mine in its thickened state in plastic food containers and defrost when needed.

Notes

a) The base gravy should be quite <u>thin</u> when cooking a BIR curry. Dilute it with an equal amount of water to get a consistency of semi-skimmed milk, and always heat it up before using it to avoid slowing the curry cooking process. When making curry I always have a saucepan with the hot diluted base gravy simmering away.
b) You can make smaller or larger amounts of base gravy by simply scaling this recipe down or up.

Base Gravy thinned out, hot, and ready to use   Photo: Rob Forsdyke

Ginger/Garlic Paste

Fresh is best if you have the time and inclination. I recommend making a good amount of ginger/garlic paste: it lasts well in the fridge if kept airtight, and it is easier to blend in larger quantities.

Firstly, trim the outer peel from the fresh ginger and then chop it into chunks. For the garlic, cut off the root end from each clove. It's easier if you take a whole garlic bulb intact and use a large knife to slice through the roots of all cloves in one action. To remove the peel, take a knife with a large blade, and with some force, squash the garlic cloves open. The skin will be easy to peel off. Chop into chunks.

Now blend all the chunks with a little oil to a smooth paste in a food processor (or a pestle & mortar). The oil makes the blending easier and serves as a preservative. Don't add water: it causes the paste to spit viciously when frying.

Ginger has a stronger flavour than garlic. I suggest using a ratio (by volume) of 2:1 or 3:1 in favour of garlic.

Refrigerate in an airtight container to have it readily available for use. It should stay fresh enough for at least a couple of weeks. You can also freeze the paste. Empty the paste into ice cube trays, freeze, then seal in a freezer bag. It should still be usable after six months.

If time is short, as I mentioned earlier you can buy frozen ginger and garlic paste blocks that are 100% pure and make life easier while being almost as good as fresh.

Tomato Paste

I refer to it many times in this book's recipes. Tomato paste can be prepared in several different ways:

- Tomato purée (double concentrated) diluted with THREE times its volume of water. For example, if a recipe calls for 4 TBSP tomato paste, mix 1 TBSP tomato purée with 3 TBSP water.

- Blend tinned or fresh tomatoes to form the paste. The tinned plum variety has more flavour than that sold as 'chopped', and fresh, ripe, vibrant red vine tomatoes are superior to bland, cheap 'salad' tomatoes. Of course, fresh tomatoes are considerably more expensive than tinned.

- Passata. No need to dilute. Avoid products with added herbs such as basil.

Pre-Cooked Chicken

This recipe yields a batch of pre-cooked chicken to be used when cooking curries. It produces about five to six generous portions of 200g. If cooked and stored properly the chicken remains tender. Boneless and skinless chicken breasts are normally used in BIR cooking, which reflects the British preference in restaurant curries. Substitute with thighs instead for a tastier, cheaper alternative with a different texture.

The recipe can be scaled up (or down) to make more.

Ingredients

- 1½kg Chicken Breasts or Thighs (trimmed, boneless and skinless)
- 1 tsp Turmeric
- Whole Spices for simmering the Chicken:
  - 3 Cloves
  - 1-2 large Bay Leaves (Asian Bay Tej Patta preferable)
  - 10-15 cm Cassia Bark
  - 3 Green Cardamoms (split open)
  - 1 tsp Fennel Seeds (optional)
- 90-120ml Oil (6-8 TBSP)
- Whole Spices for the sauce:
  - 1-2 large Bay Leaves (Asian Bay Tej Patta preferable)
  - 10-15cm Cassia Bark
- 1½ TBSP Ginger/Garlic Paste, 2 TBSP Tomato Purée, ¾ tsp Salt
- 200-300ml Base Gravy, 150-200ml Water

Method

1. Chop the chicken into even 4-6cm size pieces. Bring a large pan of water to a simmer and add the chicken, turmeric and whole spices. Simmer for 15-20 minutes for breast or 20–25 minutes for thigh. Stir occasionally.
2. Remove the chicken and soak in cold water to cool and stop the cooking process, then place into a container and cover.
3. The chicken needs an aromatic sauce to cover it and marinate it post-cooking. You can make this sauce whilst the chicken is simmering to save time.
4. Add 3-4 TBSP oil to a large frying pan on medium high heat. Throw in the bay leaves and cassia bark. Fry for 45-60 seconds, stirring to infuse the oil.
5. Add the ginger/garlic paste and stir-fry until the sizzling sound reduces.
6. Now add the tomato purée and salt. Fry for another 30-40 seconds, stirring the tomato purée into the mixture.
7. Pour in 200-300ml of base gravy and another 3-4 TBSP of oil. This extra oil will help coat the chicken pieces and keep them moist. (You can add the extra oil in at the beginning if you wish, but it can cause splattering so I prefer to add it at this stage.) Stir well, then leave to cook on high heat for 4-5 minutes with minimal interference.
8. During this time allow the sauce to reduce, but top up with extra water towards the end so that the final consistency is like a very thin curry. This is important to ensure that there is enough sauce to coat the chicken pieces.
9. Now pour the sauce over the chicken in the container. Mix gently to ensure all the chicken pieces are coated with the

sauce. Remove the whole spices when you see them.
10. Allow to cool, cover, and refrigerate. The pre-cooked chicken will keep safely for 3-4 days in the fridge. Alternatively, to freeze, empty into airtight freezer bags in individual portion sizes, making sure to use plenty of the extra sauce to coat the chicken generously. Use within 3 months.

Notes

a) Always keep raw chicken away from other ingredients, and thoroughly clean everything that has been in contact with it.
b) If scaling the recipe up to make more you will need a larger frying pan, wok, or pan to accommodate making the extra sauce.

Pre-Cooked Lamb

This recipe details how to pre-cook a batch of lamb leg or shoulder to be used subsequently in curries. It produces about five portions as well as a superb lamb stock. If cooked and stored properly, the lamb remains tender. The recipe can be simply scaled up (or down) as desired, and you can substitute lamb with mutton, beef, or even goat.

Ingredients

- 1kg Lamb Leg or Shoulder (boneless weight, chopped in 3-4cm pieces) and any bones going spare
- 125-150ml Oil (Vegetable/Sunflower, etc.)
- 1 Star Anise, 10cm Cassia Bark, 2 large Asian Bay Leaves (optional. You can use European Bay Leaves instead), 1 tsp Cumin Seeds, 1 Black Cardamom split open (optional)
- 150-175g Onion, very finely chopped or puréed (about 2 medium Onions), 1½ TBSP Ginger/Garlic Paste
- 2 TBSP Mix Powder, 2 tsp Curry Powder (e.g. Mild Madras), 1 TBSP Paprika, 1-1½ tsp Salt, 1½ tsp Kasuri Methi
- 3 TBSP Tomato Purée (double concentrated) + a splash of water

Method

1. Ensure that the lamb is deboned, trimmed of excess sinew/fat, and chopped into 3-4 cm pieces (a good butcher will gladly do this for you). Ask to keep the spare bones.
2. In a large pan (preferably metal) heat up the oil on medium high heat. Throw in the star anise, cassia, Asian bay, cumin seeds, and the optional black cardamom.
3. Fry for 45-60 seconds to infuse the oil, stirring diligently.
4. Add the onion and fry for a couple of minutes until soft and translucent but not browned. Stir frequently. Then add the ginger/garlic paste and continue to fry until the sizzling subsides, stirring frequently.
5. Now add the mix powder, curry powder, paprika, and salt. Cook for 30-45 seconds to allow the powdered spices to cook through, stirring constantly.
6. Next, add the tomato purée, methi, and a little water to loosen the mixture. Stir for a further minute.

7. Add the lamb, coat well, and cook for a further 2-3 minutes until the meat is sealed and well coated with the sauce.
8. Add 600-750ml water to cover the meat and add any spare lamb bones you have. The bones will give a great flavour to the liquid. Bring back up to a simmer, cover loosely, turn heat to low, and leave to simmer gently for 1 hour, stirring a couple of times.
9. After 1 hour test the lamb for tenderness. If it's still firm and rubbery, cook for a further 15 minutes then retest and repeat if necessary.
10. Remove the lamb meat (not the bones) from the pan into a container, and coat well with the sauce, which helps it stay moist and adds additional flavour. The pre-cooked lamb is now ready to use in curries. Discard the whole spices.
11. If not using imminently, allow to cool, cover, and refrigerate. It will keep for 3-4 days in the fridge. Alternatively, to freeze, empty into airtight freezer bags in individual portion sizes, making sure to use plenty of the extra sauce to coat the lamb generously. Use within 3 months.
12. KEEP THE REMAINING LIQUID. It will make a delicious stock which adds even more flavour to curries. Continue simmering with the lid off for a further 1-2 hours, adding extra water as required. At the end the stock should have thickened somewhat, and when cool should have a gelatinous quality. Store in the fridge for a few days or freeze in ice cube trays.

Notes

a) Always keep raw meat away from other ingredients, and thoroughly clean everything that has been in contact with it.
b) At the end of cooking the 'seasoned' oil can be salvaged with a spoon from the top of the liquid and is ideal for starting to cook meat curries with.

Succulent, tangy, magical chunks with a careful balance of spices and herbs. My recipe may seem involved, but it has proved extremely popular and it also works brilliantly in place of ordinary chicken in curries. This recipe can also be used to make starter portions of chicken tikka, and I would suggest adding a little extra seasoning (salt or chaat masala) sprinkled on top when serving.

This recipe makes enough chicken tikka for approximately seven to eight single portion curries, and can easily serve six people as a generous starter. You can scale the ingredients up or down to make more or less at a time.

Ingredients

- 1½kg Chicken Breasts or Thighs, boneless and skinless
- 1 TBSP Ginger/Garlic Paste, 1 TBSP Lemon Juice, 2 TBSP Mustard Oil, 120ml Natural Yoghurt (full fat)
- 2 tsp Coriander Seeds and 1 tsp Cumin Seeds, both freshly toasted and ground to a powder
- ½ tsp Fenugreek Seeds, ground to a powder

- 3½ TBSP Tandoori Masala, 1 tsp Turmeric, 1 tsp Kashmiri Chilli Powder, 1 TBSP Paprika,
- ¼ tsp Black Pepper, freshly ground, ½ tsp Elachi Powder (ground seeds from Green Cardamom Pods)
- 2 tsp Kasuri Methi, 1½ tsp Dried Mint, 1½ tsp Salt, ½ tsp Nutmeg, grated (optional)
- ¼ tsp Orange or Red Food Colouring (optional)
- 1 TBSP Butter Ghee, melted (optional)

Method

1. Trim the chicken of excess fat and chop into large chunks, e.g. 5cm diameter.
2. Place in a large bowl and add the ginger/garlic paste and lemon juice. Mix well with hands and leave to marinate in the fridge for 30–60 minutes.
3. Add all the other ingredients. Mix thoroughly again. Cover bowl with foil or cling film and leave to marinate in the fridge for a minimum of 4 hours, and up to 48 hours. The longer the better, so I suggest 48 hours if you have time. Stir the contents of the bowl at least once during the marinating time.
4. Remove from fridge an hour or so before the planned cooking time to allow the chicken to return to room temperature.
5. Pre-heat your grill to its highest temperature. Take a large baking tray or grill pan, cover with aluminium foil and brush lightly with oil. Place the chicken pieces on the tray, evenly spaced. You will need to cook them in two or more batches, depending how big your grill pan is.
6. Place under the pre-heated grill and cook for 5-7 minutes, until the top of the chicken starts blackening.
7. Brush the top of each piece with a little oil, turn each piece over, and brush the other side also.
8. Place back under the grill and cook again for 5-7 minutes. Cut a large piece in half to make sure it is completely cooked (no pink on the inside) and cook for a couple more minutes if needed.

Notes

a) Always keep raw chicken away from other ingredients, and thoroughly clean everything that has been in contact with it.
b) Chicken breast meat is the most commonly used for chicken tikka, but thigh meat is a slightly cheaper and flavoursome alternative.
c) It's important to baste the chicken pieces with oil. It helps keep the tikka from drying out.
d) Orange or red food colouring is optional, but it will improve the appearance.
e) If freezing, place into freezer bags and seal well. I usually bag up each single portion (4-6 pieces), and seal with a knot. Allow to cool before putting in the freezer.

Prawn Puri

Prawn puri is a classic starter dish served in Indian restaurants throughout the UK. ('Puri' is sometimes misspelt as 'puree'.) Essentially, it's a thick bhuna curry served on or in a deep-fried chapati. There's something about the combination of sweet prawns, condensed tasty sauce, soft chewy bread and a squeeze of lemon or lime that make it an absolute pleasure to consume.

This recipe will produce one very generous starter-sized portion, but is enough to happily whet the appetites of two people.

Ingredients

- 3 TBSP (45ml) Oil
- 5cm Cassia Bark
- 60g Onion, very finely chopped
- 1-1½ tsp Ginger/Garlic Paste
- ½-1 tsp Kasuri Methi
- ¾-1 tsp Mix Powder
- ¼ tsp Salt
- ¼ tsp Chilli Powder (optional)
- 200ml+ Base Gravy, heated up
- 2 TBSP Tomato Paste
- 120-150g Prawns (defrosted, pre-cooked or raw)
- 1 tsp of Lemon or Lime Juice (optional)
- 1-2 fresh Tomato Segments
- 1 TBSP of fresh Coriander Leaves, finely chopped
- 1 Puri (fried Chapati)
- A Wedge of Lemon or Lime
- Fresh Coriander for garnishing

Method

1. Add the oil to a frying pan on medium high heat.
2. When hot, add the cassia bark and fry for 30–45 seconds to infuse the oil, stirring occasionally.
3. Add the chopped onion. Fry for 1-1½ minutes until soft, stirring often.
4. Then add the ginger/garlic paste and fry for a further 20-30 seconds whilst continuing to stir frequently.
5. Next throw in the kasuri methi, mix powder, salt and the optional chilli powder. Be careful with the salt – the prawns will be salty already.
6. Fry for 20-30 seconds, adding a little base gravy (e.g. 30ml) if and when the spices start to stick to the pan. Stir diligently.
7. Turn up the heat to high and pour in the tomato paste. Stir together and let fry for 20-30 seconds or until the oil separates and small craters appear around the edges of the frying pan.
8. Next add 75ml of base gravy. Stir the sauce and leave on high heat until the sauce has reduced a little, the oil has separated, and small craters form around the edges again.
9. Then add about 100ml of base gravy. Stir and scrape the pan once then leave it to cook on high heat for 2-2½ minutes. Avoid stirring unless the curry is about to burn - let the sauce stick to the bottom and sides of the pan to caramelise and thicken. Add extra base gravy if desired, but make sure to reduce it down so the end result is very thick.
10. Add the prawns and the tomato segments. Stir together and let cook for an additional 2 minutes or until the prawns have cooked through. Larger prawns will take a minute or so longer.

11. Remove the cassia bark and stir in the fresh coriander.

12. Serve on top of a warm puri (see below), and garnish with a sprinkling of fresh coriander and a wedge of lemon or lime.

The Puri

1. Take a small or medium-sized cooked chapati (see Notes) and deep-fry it in hot oil at a temperature of about 180°C for 30 seconds, turning it over half way through. You can instead shallow fry it in about 1cm depth of hot oil for the same amount of time.

2. Scoop the puri out of the oil and drain the excess oil. Place it between two pieces of kitchen towel to soak up more of the oil and to help keep it warm before serving up.

3. For a healthier option you can skip the deep-frying step and just use a warm chapati instead.

Notes

a) Larger sized prawns may be substituted for the usual small variety but do ensure they are thoroughly cooked before eating with no translucency in the middle.

b) An easy chapati recipe is included in Volume 1.

c) Make sure to scrape out all the residue from the bottom and sides of the pan when you are serving. There's a lot of fantastic flavour in the thick crusty bits.

d) Overindulging in this compelling prawn puri can spoil your appetite for the main course. Eat wisely!

Achari Chicken Tikka

This special recipe leads chicken astray from the typical chicken tikka with different dimensions of spice. Achari chicken tikka features Indian pickle, lemon juice, a special masala containing pickling spices, and is packed with layers of tangy flavour. It's excellent cooked as a kebab on a charcoal barbecue for a smoky taste, and of course can also be cooked in your kitchen.

The recipe makes enough for about three to four starter size portions. To make more you can simply scale the ingredients up.

Ingredients

- 500-600g Boneless Chicken Breast or Thighs, trimmed of excess fat and cut into 4-5cm pieces
- 3 TBSP Natural Yoghurt (full fat)
- 2-3 TBSP Lemon Juice
- 2-3 TBSP Ginger/Garlic Paste
- 2 TBSP Indian Pickle, mashed or chopped until smooth. Suggested types of Pickle: Lime, Mango, Mixed, Chilli, Garlic, Naga
- 2-3 tsp Mango Chutney, mashed or chopped until smooth (optional)
- 1-2 TBSP Mustard Oil (optional)
- A pinch of Yellow Food Colouring (optional)
- Spice Blend (grind the whole spices into a powder):
    - ½ tsp Fenugreek Seeds
    - 1 tsp Cumin Seeds
    - 1 tsp Fennel Seeds
    - 1½ tsp Black Mustard Seeds
    - ½ tsp Kalonji Seeds (aka Nigella)
    - 1 tsp Turmeric Powder
    - ¾ tsp Salt
    - 1-2 tsp Kashmiri Chilli Powder (optional, for a little heat and colour)
- 3-4 TBSP Oil plus extra for basting
- 2 TBSP Tomato Purée (double concentrated)

Method

1. To a bowl add the yoghurt, lemon juice, ginger/garlic paste, mashed pickle, the chicken pieces, and optionally, the mango chutney, mustard oil, and/or yellow food colouring. Mix together thoroughly, cover and refrigerate for 20-30 minutes.
2. Meanwhile, prepare the spice blend by grinding the whole spices and adding the turmeric, salt, and optional Kashmiri chilli powder.
3. Heat 3-4 TBSP oil in a frying pan (non-stick is OK for this) on medium high heat.
4. Add the spice blend, cook and stir for 30 seconds, then mix in the tomato purée with a splash of water.
5. Continue cooking for 1 minute, stirring constantly.
6. Turn off the heat and allow to cool down for a few minutes.
7. Empty the cooked spice blend mixture over the chicken and mix very well. A silicone spatula is useful to scoop out any residue from the pan.
8. Cover and refrigerate for at least 4 hours. Overnight is better, but 48 hours will give optimal results.
9. Remove the chicken marinade mixture from the fridge and leave for 30 minutes before grilling. If you are cooking outside on a BBQ, I recommend sliding the chicken pieces onto metal kebab skewers.
10. Add a little extra oil to the leftover marinade mixture to baste the chicken before and during cooking.

11. For the kitchen grill/griddle: Wipe the grill rack with a little oil, which will help stop the chicken pieces from sticking. Preheat the grill to about 180°C / 360°F and cook for 20-25 minutes (for thigh) or 15-20 minutes (for breast). Turn once during that time.
12. For the BBQ: Wipe the surface of the BBQ grill area with a little oil to help stop the chicken from sticking. Instead (and preferably), use a rack to elevate the kebabs so they don't touch the grill. Let the BBQ come up to a medium heat and cook for 20-25 minutes (thigh) or 15-20 minutes (breast), turning a few times during cooking, brushing on the spare marinade to keep the chicken moist.
13. Whichever method you use, make sure that you baste the chicken pieces well before and during cooking. Most importantly, ensure the chicken is cooked thoroughly by cutting open the largest piece of the chicken to check for any pink or translucent bits in the centre. If in doubt, cook for a further few minutes or until there is no sign of rawness.
14. Serve with wedges of lemon, mint raita, and fresh green salad. Delicious!

Notes

a) When skewering the chicken pieces, intersperse with chunks of red/green pepper, mushrooms, courgettes and onion for a delicious mixed kebab. Before skewering, season the vegetables in a little oil, salt, ginger/garlic paste, and kasuri methi for a nice flavour.
b) When handling raw chicken make sure all work surfaces, hands, utensils, etc. are cleaned properly afterwards.
c) There are a few minor differences over the accompanying YouTube recipe video. Indian pickle increased to 2 TBSP, added optional mango chutney for a hint of sweetness, optional yellow food colouring for vibrancy, and mustard oil for tang.

Malai Chicken Tikka

This is something a little bit different, and is a style of tikka you are unlikely to find on the menus of most British Indian Restaurants or takeaways. Boneless chicken is marinated in mild, aromatic spices, cream/yoghurt and cheese, then skewered and grilled.

Malai chicken tikka is popular in India. I first encountered these delicious kebabs in a bar in Mumbai in 2016, and vowed to create a recipe in the Misty Ricardo style. Enjoy!

The recipe makes enough for about three to four starter size portions. To make more you can simply scale the ingredients up.

Ingredients

- 500-600g Boneless Chicken Thighs, trimmed of excess fat and cut into 4-5cm pieces
- 2 TBSP Ginger/Garlic Paste
- 1½ TBSP Lemon Juice
- ¼ tsp Salt
- ½-¾ tsp Garam Masala
- 1 tsp Elachi Powder or the ground seeds from 6-10 Green Cardamom Pods
- ¼-½ tsp Ground Black Pepper
- 100g Cream Cheese
- 120g Grated Cheese. I use 60g of Mozzarella and 60g of Cheddar, a good contrast of strong, mild, and stringy
- 60g Double Cream or Natural Yoghurt (full fat)
- 4-5 TBSP Cornflour or Rice Flour
- A small handful of Coriander Stalks and Leaves, very finely chopped or minced
- 1-2 Green Chillies, minced (optional)
- 1-2 TBSP Oil for basting
- A sprinkle of Chaat Masala (optional)

Method

1. Add the ginger/garlic paste, lemon juice, salt, garam masala, elachi/cardamom, and black pepper to a bowl. Add the chicken pieces, mix together thoroughly, cover and refrigerate for at least 20-30 minutes.
2. Put the cream cheese, grated cheese(s), cream or yoghurt, the minced/finely chopped coriander, and optional minced chilli into a separate bowl.
3. Crush the mixture forcefully using a fork or a potato masher to break up and incorporate the grated cheese with the other ingredients.
4. Add the cornflour or rice flour to thicken the mixture and help the marinade stick to the chicken. Mix and mash it together well. It may seem overly thick, but that's what is needed.
5. Combine the contents of the chicken bowl with the main marinade mixture, ensuring the chicken is fully coated. A silicone spatula is useful to scoop out any residual marinade.
6. Cover and refrigerate for at least 4 hours. Overnight is better, but 48 hours gives optimal results.
7. Before cooking remove the chicken marinade mixture from the fridge and weave the thigh pieces onto metal skewers. Run the skewer through at least three parts of each thigh piece to create folds for the marinade to cling to. Let any excess marinade fall off and then leave for 15-30 minutes. Add a little extra oil to the leftover marinade mixture to baste the kebabs during cooking.
8. Wipe the grill rack with a little oil to prevent the chicken pieces sticking while cooking. Pre-heat the grill to about 180°C, place the skewers onto the grill rack, and cook for 20-25 minutes.
9. Turn once during that time, and brush more of the marinade on. If you don't want to waste the extra marinade, spoon it generously onto the chicken a minute or two before the end of cooking. Some of the marinade will inevitably drip down onto the grill pan, and lining the grill pan with foil is a good way to retain it. After cooking the crusty semi-burnt bits can be gently levered off the foil with a spatula (lots of flavour).
10. Make sure the chicken is cooked throughout. Cut open the largest piece of the chicken to check for any pink or translucent bits in the centre. If in doubt, cook for a further 5 minutes or until there is no sign of pink bits.
11. Serve with salad and an optional sprinkling of chaat masala for extra tang.

Notes

a) When handling raw chicken make sure that work surfaces, utensils and hands are cleaned properly afterwards.
b) If you still have any leftover marinade after the end of cooking, remember it has been in contact with raw chicken, so should be cooked properly before eating. Suggested use: chop up some vegetables (e.g. onion, pepper, mushroom, tomato, courgette, etc.), coat with the marinade and cook tasty vegetable kebabs. Another suggestion: spread on top of a burger a few minutes before the end of cooking.
c) This recipe has had a few minor changes since the associated YouTube video was published: a little more spice to compensate for any wasted marinade, and more cornflour/rice flour to hold the marinade together better.

Keema Peas

A lush and delicious side dish that's very moreish. Minced lamb and green peas join forces for a savoury and slightly sweet oral ecstasy experience. You only have to imagine scooping up a delicious dollop of keema peas with a crispy naan bread to make you head straight to the kitchen to cook this dish. Leftovers (if any at all) are fantastic eaten cold from the fridge the next day. Try it!

Being quite rich, this recipe will easily serve two to three people as a side dish.

Ingredients

- 2–3 TBSP (30-45ml) Oil
- 75g Onion, roughly chopped
- 1½ tsp Ginger/Garlic Paste
- 1 tsp Kasuri Methi
- 1 tsp Mix Powder
- ¼ tsp Turmeric
- ¼ tsp Garam Masala
- ¼-½ tsp Salt
- ¼ tsp Chilli Powder (optional)
- 1 TBSP Coriander Stalks, very finely chopped
- 255ml+ Base Gravy, heated up
- 200g Pre-cooked Keema (see Notes)
- 120g Peas, defrosted
- 2 Tomato Quarters
- 1-2 fresh Green Chillies, finely chopped (optional)
- Coriander Leaf to garnish, finely chopped

Method

1. Add the oil to a frying pan on medium high heat.
2. When hot, add the onion and fry for 1½-2 minutes until the onions are translucent and showing signs of starting to brown.
3. Now add the ginger/garlic paste and fry until the sizzling reduces. Stir frequently.
4. Next add the kasuri methi, mix powder, turmeric, garam masala, salt, and optionally the chilli powder.
5. Fry for 20-30 seconds, stirring diligently. Quench with a splash of base gravy (e.g. 30ml) if the spices start to stick to the pan, to help them cook without burning.
6. Add the pre-cooked keema and the coriander stalks. Mix well into the sauce.
7. Turn up heat to high and add 75ml of base gravy. Stir once and leave untampered for 45 seconds or until the sauce thickens up a bit, and you can see increased surface oil and small craters around the edges of the pan.
8. Add a second 75ml of base and repeat the previous step.
9. Add the final 75-100ml of base gravy, the peas, tomato quarters, and the optional fresh chilli. Stir and scrape once when first added then leave to cook on high heat for 3-5 minutes, or until the desired consistency is reached. Resist stirring and allow the sauce to caramelise and stick to the bottom and sides of the pan, but do not allow to burn. Add a little extra base gravy near the end of cooking to thin things out if desired.
10. Garnish with the coriander leaves on top.

Notes

a) The recipe calls for keema that has been pre-cooked for the convenience of speedy cooking. You can use raw mince instead – just add it in after the oil is hot with ½ tsp mix powder and a bay leaf. Fry on medium heat for 8-10 minutes before continuing with the recipe at the onion stage. Adjust salt to taste at the end of cooking.

b) A comprehensive recipe for pre-cooked keema is included in Volume 1, the prequel to this book.

Starters & Sides

Chicken Pakoras

Pakoras are a particularly popular Indian restaurant/takeaway snack in Scotland, especially in the central belt area of Glasgow and Edinburgh. In essence pakoras are crispy deep-fried nuggets of spiced chicken or onion/vegetables/haggis in a thick gram (chickpea) flour batter. They are usually served with a pink, sweet and tangy sauce.

This recipe was generously provided by my chef and actor friend Alex Wilkie, who has spent a lot of time working in an Indian takeaway near Glasgow. BIR food in Scotland differs significantly from that in other regions of the UK, tending to be a little richer and sweeter. I can imagine how good these chicken pakoras must taste as a late-night takeaway supper after being out on a cold, dark Scottish evening.

The 1kg of chicken breasts used in this recipe yield six to eight starter/snack-size portions. Simply scale up or down to make more or less.

Ingredients

Pakoras

- 1kg Chicken Breasts, boneless and skinless
- 1½ tsp Salt
- ½ tsp Chilli Powder
- 1 tsp Garam Masala
- 1¾ TBSP Ginger/Garlic Paste
- 20-30ml Lemon Juice
- 1¾ TBSP Tandoori Paste (commercial brand)
- ½ tsp Orange Food Colouring (optional)
- Gram Flour (Chick Pea Flour, Besan. Approx. 60g, or enough to form a thick batter)

Pakora Sauce

- 200g Natural Yoghurt (full fat)
- 5-6 TBSP Tomato Ketchup
- 1¼ TBSP Mango Chutney, smoothed out of any lumps
- 1-2 tsp Mint Sauce,
- ¼ tsp Chilli Powder
- ¼ tsp Red Food Colouring
- 1 tsp White Sugar
- Milk (to thin the sauce)

Method

1. Chop the chicken breasts into thick strips about 4cm long and 2cm wide. Try to keep each piece about the same size.
2. Place the chicken pieces into a large bowl with the salt, chilli powder, garam masala, ginger/garlic paste, lemon juice, tandoori paste, and the orange food colouring.
3. Mix well and set aside for a minimum of 2 hours. It's better to marinate overnight in the fridge, but before proceeding to fry make sure the mixture is not 'fridge-cold'.
4. To batter the chicken first add about 30g of gram flour, a little water, then mix together. Then add another 30g of gram flour with some more water and mix again. You are aiming for a thick smooth batter which sticks to the chicken but does not drip off when lifted out of the bowl.
5. Heat a medium-large pan half-filled (no more) with oil to 160°C. A laser gun or a cooking thermometer is useful to measure the exact temperature of the

Starters & Sides

oil. Alternatively, use a deep fat fryer if you have one.

6. The chicken pakoras need to be cooked in 3-4 batches to avoid overcrowding the pan. If too much is placed in the oil the temperature will drop too far, and the batter will not stick to the chicken.
7. Place each batch of the battered chicken (I suggest a quarter of the mixture per batch) gently into the hot oil. Allow to settle for a few seconds then gently stir with a heat-resistant spoon.
8. Leave to deep-fry for 10 minutes, stirring once or twice during that time.
9. The oil needs to be kept at a minimum temperature of about 135°C. Any lower and there is a strong possibility the batter will separate from the pakora pieces. Likewise keep the temperature below 160°C. The chicken needs to be thoroughly cooked inside whilst not burning the outside.
10. After the 10 minutes scoop out the largest size pakora and cut it in half. The inside should be all white. If not then continue frying for a further few minutes and retest another piece of chicken.
11. Scoop out the cooked pakoras and drain on kitchen towel. Repeat for the remaining batches.
12. Best eaten immediately while still hot and crispy. Warning: these are very addictive!

Pakora Sauce

1. Mix all the sauce ingredients together thoroughly, using a little milk to help thin the sauce to a consistency suitable for dipping into. It should be a nice pink colour.

Notes

a) The pakoras will lose their crispness if left uneaten. To restore them to their former glory, place them on a baking tray in a preheated hot oven for 5-10 minutes or deep-fry at 180°C for a few minutes.

b) Boneless chicken thigh can be used instead of breast in this recipe. The firmer but more flavoursome thigh meat will take a little longer to deep-fry so it's cooked throughout.

c) The use of shop-bought spice pastes (for example Patak's, Pasco, Laziza) is common in most Indian restaurants and takeaways in the UK. Generally speaking they are used mostly for convenience in marinades. This recipe exhibits a typical example of how the convenience of a commercial paste can be used (in moderation) to enhance flavour.

d) Always keep raw chicken away from other ingredients and thoroughly clean everything that has been in contact with it before and after cooking with it.

e) For reasons that should be obvious, care and attention is needed when deep-frying. Do not leave the pakoras frying unattended.

f) The orange food colouring is optional but gives the pakoras a great look.

Vegetable Samosa

These golden crunchy triangles of joy are filled with a potato, onion, and pea masala mixture. I think the fennel seeds and the amchoor powder go very well in these vegetable samosas.

This recipe will make about 12 samosas that will feed at least six people as a starter or side dish.

The ingredients can be scaled up or down uniformly as desired, and the filling can be frozen once cooked and used later.

Ingredients

- 2 TBSP (30ml) Oil
- 2 tsp Cumin Seeds
- ½ tsp Fennel Seeds
- 100g Onion, finely chopped
- 1½ tsp Garlic, finely chopped
- 2 tsp Ginger, finely chopped
- 1 tsp Coriander Powder
- ½ tsp Garam Masala
- 1 tsp Turmeric
- ¼ tsp Black Pepper
- ¾-1 tsp Salt
- 1 tsp Kashmiri Chilli Powder (optional)
- 80g Peas, defrosted
- 160g Potato, boiled and chopped into very small pieces (peeled weight)
- 2 TBSP fresh Coriander Stalks and Leaves, finely chopped
- 3-4 Green Chillies, finely chopped (optional)
- ¾ tsp Amchoor (unripe mango) Powder or 1-2 tsp Lemon Juice. Either is optional.
- 2 tsp Mango Chutney (optional)
- Filo or Wonton Wrappers (available in supermarkets refrigerated or frozen)

Method

1. Firstly peel and boil the potatoes, drain, allow to cool, and chop into very small pieces.
2. Add the oil to a frying pan on medium heat.
3. When the oil is hot add the cumin and fennel seeds, and fry until the cumin seeds start to sizzle.
4. Add the onion and fry for 1-2 minutes, stirring often.
5. Next add the chopped garlic and ginger and continue frying for another minute, stirring frequently.
6. Add the coriander powder, garam masala, turmeric, black pepper, salt, and the optional Kashmiri chilli powder. (Regular chilli powder is fine to use – just use about half the amount.)
7. Fry the mixture for a 1-2 minutes, stirring constantly. Add a little water to prevent the spices burning.
8. Now put in the peas, potato, fresh coriander, and optional green chillies. Mix well and cook for a further 2-3 minutes until the filling mixture is dry. Add a little water during cooking if it dries out too much, to prevent burning.
9. Add the amchoor powder (dried mango powder) or lemon juice (optional).
10. Taste and adjust seasoning. If you prefer a slightly sweet filling add the mango chutney.
11. The filling should be dry so that it doesn't make the pastry soggy. Turn off the heat and wait for the mixture to cool down before starting to assemble the samosas.

Vegetable Samosas

12. To make each samosa, carefully place down a single square wonton wrapper sheet on a clean, dry surface, and cut it into 2 or 3 strips horizontally. The width of each strip will determine the size of the samosas.
13. Place a dollop of the filling near one end of one of the strips, and fold the pastry from the corner to form a covered triangle at that end.
14. Now, fold that triangle into the pastry strip. Repeat the folding until all the strip has been wrapped around the triangular samosa.
15. Seal the edge of the end of the pastry onto the samosa with a little water or cornflour slurry, so that it does not unravel during frying.
16. Repeat, wrapping as many samosas as you want, or until the filling runs out. You can store any leftover filling in the fridge or freezer for later use.
17. Deep-fry the samosa at 180°C for 1 minute each side, or until the pastry has turned golden brown.
18. As a healthier alternative you can instead bake the samosas. Brush a bit of oil on both sides of each samosa, then place on a baking tray in a preheated oven at 180°C for 10 minutes, turning them over half way through, or until the samosas are golden brown.
19. Serve with your choice of dips, such as mint, tamarind, ketchup, raita, etc.

Notes

a) You could use a double layer of the filo pastry for a thicker samosa. The doubling up makes them easier to fold, but make sure you cook them for long enough so that the inner layer gets browned. A slightly lower oil temperature will help ensure the samosas don't burn on the outside before being cooked within.

b) Folding samosas takes some practice. The ones you see in the recipe photograph had predecessors that were very strange shapes indeed!

Brinjal Bhaji

Brinjal is the Hindi word for aubergine or eggplant, and brinjal bhaji is an ingenious starter or side dish that is sadly overlooked. You would be forgiven for thinking this is a crispy dish, like onion bhaji. Traditionally, a bhaji or bhaaji comprises vegetables fried in batter, but restaurants have applied the term to a range of starter and side dishes on their menus. Brinjal bhaji is one of the more popular ones, and for good reason.

Thick, dry, but juicy and full of flavour, the aubergine soaks up a lot of flavour, and its soft texture is pleasing in the mouth. Panch phoran and lemon juice help to give the brinjal bhaji a characteristic taste.

Ingredients

- 3½-4½ TBSP Oil (1½ TBSP for the Aubergine fry, 2-3 TBSP for the main dish)
- 200g Aubergine, cubed
- ½ tsp Cumin Seeds
- 1 tsp Panch Phoran
- 75g Onion, finely chopped
- 2 Garlic Cloves, finely sliced
- 1¼ tsp Ginger/Garlic Paste
- 1 tsp Kasuri Methi
- 1¼ tsp Mix Powder
- ¼ tsp Turmeric
- ½ tsp Salt (¼ tsp for the Aubergine fry and ¼ tsp for the main dish)
- Pinch of Garam Masala (about one eighth of a tsp)
- ¼ tsp Chilli Powder (optional)
- 180m+ Base Gravy, heated up
- 3 TBSP Tomato Paste
- 1 tsp Lemon Juice
- 1 medium Tomato, halved and sliced
- Fresh Coriander Leaves for garnishing

Method

1. Firstly, to pre-cook the aubergine, add 1½ TBSP of the oil to a wok, korai, or frying pan on high heat.
2. Add the aubergine cubes and ¼ tsp of the salt. Fry for a minute or two, stirring frequently, until the cubes are slightly browned but still firm. Empty and keep to one side.
3. Pour in the remainder of the oil (2½-3½ TBSP) to the same cooking vessel, and bring to medium high heat.
4. Add the cumin seeds and panch phoran. Fry for 30-45 seconds to infuse flavour into the oil, or until the mustard seeds start popping. Stir diligently.
5. Next add the finely chopped onion. Fry for around 60–90 seconds, then add the thinly sliced garlic and cook for a further 30 seconds, or until the garlic slices brown around the edges. Stir avidly to stop anything from sticking to the pan and burning.
6. Add the ginger/garlic paste and continue to cook for 15-30 seconds or until the paste quietens down with less sizzling. Stir often.
7. Now add the kasuri methi, mix powder, turmeric, garam masala, salt, and the optional chilli powder.
8. Fry for 20-30 seconds, stirring diligently. The powdered spices will want to stick to the pan surface. Let that happen, briefly, but add a splash (e.g. 30ml) of base gravy to give the spices enough time to cook properly without burning.
9. Add the tomato paste and the pre-cooked aubergine. Turn up the heat to high and mix everything together.
10. Then pour in 75ml of base gravy, stir into the sauce, and leave on high heat with no further stirring until the sauce has reduced a little, and small craters form around the edges.
11. Now add a second 75ml of base gravy and the sliced tomatoes. Stir and scrape the bottom and sides of the pan once when first added, then allow the sauce to cook down for 3-4 minutes.
12. Stir and scrape once or twice to mix the caramelised sauce back in, but do this only to prevent the sauce from sticking too much and burning.
13. It's important to let the mixture stick to the bottom and sides of the pan, which caramelises it and gives a magnificent flavour. The brinjal bhaji is supposed to be a thick dish, but add extra base gravy if you think the sauce is thickening up too much.
14. Just before serving, mix in the finely chopped fresh coriander leaves.
15. Serve, garnishing with extra fresh coriander if desired.

Notes

a) Panch phoran (spelling differs) is a mixture of five different spice seeds: cumin, fennel, fenugreek, black mustard, and nigella (kalonji), usually in equal proportions. You can buy it from South Asian groceries and some mainstream supermarkets.

Mushroom Bhaji

Mushrooms come into their own in this simple but delicious side dish. Browning them on high heat at the beginning of cooking caramelises them and intensifies the flavour. Try adding a little Worcestershire sauce, which complements the mushroom bhaji nicely.

This recipe serves two to three as a side dish.

Ingredients

- 3 TBSP (45ml) Oil
- 200g Mushrooms, sliced
- 50g Onion, very finely chopped
- ¼ tsp Salt
- 1¼ tsp Ginger/Garlic Paste
- ½ tsp Kasuri Methi
- 1 tsp Mix Powder
- ¼ tsp Chilli Powder (optional)
- 180ml Base Gravy, heated up
- 2 TBSP Tomato Paste
- A few dashes of Worcestershire Sauce (optional)
- 1 TBSP of finely chopped fresh Coriander Leaves

Method

1. Add the oil to a frying pan on high heat.
2. When the oil is hot, add the chopped onion, mushroom slices, and the salt.
3. Fry for 1–2 minutes until the mushrooms have reduced in size and browned slightly. Stir frequently.
4. Then add the ginger/garlic paste and fry for a further, 20-30 seconds, continuing to stir frequently.
5. Now add the kasuri methi, mix powder, and the optional chilli powder.
6. Fry for 20-30 seconds, adding a splash of base gravy (e.g. 30ml) if the spices start to stick to the pan. Stir very often and use the base of the spoon to ensure flat and even distribution of the spices.
7. Next add the tomato paste. Stir together and leave for 20-30 seconds or until the oil separates and small craters appear around the edges of the frying pan.
8. Now add 75ml of base gravy. Stir everything together and leave to cook on high heat until the sauce has reduced a little, the oil has separated, and small craters form around the edges again.
9. Add a second 75ml of base gravy and the optional Worcestershire sauce. Stir and scrape the pan once, then leave to cook for a couple of minutes until the sauce is very thick.
10. Add the fresh coriander then mix everything together. Make sure you scrape the sticky caramelised sauce back into the bhaji. Adjust salt to taste.
11. Serve garnished with a sprinkle of fresh coriander.

Notes

a) When emptying the curry from the frying pan, ensure you include all the residue from the bottom and sides too. There's a lot of amazing flavour in the thick bits.
b) If using Worcestershire sauce, bear in mind that it contains anchovy, which is non-vegetarian. Vegetarian-friendly brands are available, such as Henderson's, Biona and Chippa.

Bhindi Fry

Please stop right there before you turn the page - this dish might change your life! OK, it probably won't do that, but I hope you will be glad you tried my recipe.

Bhindi fry is excellent as a side dish alongside contrasting curries, and it makes an interesting change from the norm. It's a dry dish packed with layers of flavour, and the okra has a pleasing texture.

I have created this recipe to be of a more 'desi' style, and it does not require base gravy. In fact there are no onions, garlic, or ginger in it either, but despite that it's very robust and flavoursome.

Bhindi (okra) has a reputation for being a slimy vegetable, however this can be mostly avoided with a few techniques.

This recipe will serve two to three people as a side dish, or it can be eaten by itself by one happy vegan or vegetarian (it's very good with chapatis).

Ingredients

- 250g Okra
- 3 TBSP (45ml) Oil. Use a 50/50 Mustard/Vegetable Oil combination for more flavour
- ½ tsp Cumin Seeds
- ¾ tsp Black Mustard Seeds
- ¼ tsp Fenugreek Seeds
- ½ tsp Hing (a.k.a. Asafoetida. See Notes)
- ½ tsp Garam Masala
- ¼-½ tsp Kashmiri Chilli Powder
- ¼ tsp Turmeric
- 2 tsp Coriander Seeds and 1 tsp Cumin Seeds, both dry-toasted in a pan then ground to a powder
- 3 TBSP Tomato Paste
- 1-2 tsp Lemon Juice or ¾ tsp Amchoor (dried unripe mango powder)
- 90ml+ Water
- ¼-½ tsp Salt

Method

1. Wash the okra and thoroughly pat it dry with paper towels. Slice each okra widthwise into 3-4cm pentangles. Chop them no thinner than that to reduce the risk of sliminess.
2. Now toast and grind the coriander and cumin seeds, then set aside.
3. Add the oil to a frying pan on medium high heat.
4. When the oil is hot, add the cumin seeds, mustard seeds, fenugreek seeds, and the hing. Fry for 30-40 seconds or until the mustard seeds start to pop, stirring frequently.
5. Next add the garam masala, chilli powder, turmeric, and the ground cumin and coriander.
6. Stir continually for 20-30 seconds, adding a splash of water or vegetable stock when the powdered spices start to cling to the pan. This will allow them enough time to cook properly without burning.
7. Turn the heat up to high and add the tomato paste (remember this is 1 part tomato purée mixed with 3 parts water).
8. Cook for 30 seconds, stirring occasionally.
9. Now add the lemon/amchoor and the okra chunks. Mix everything together and fry for a minute before stirring in 3 TBSP (45ml) of water. The acid content of the lemon/amchoor is very important as it will curtail the bhindi's viscous nature.
10. Leave to cook for 5-6 minutes, stirring very occasionally. The bhindi fry is a dry dish, but you will need to add a little extra water during cooking to stop it drying out too much and burning. When you do add more water, add it in small amounts of no more than 3 TBSP at a time. It's important that the bhindi is frying more so than boiling. Excess water encourages it to steam, which causes the undesirable sliminess to ooze out.
11. Now add the salt and cook for a further 1-2 minutes. The salt is added now rather than near the beginning, so as not to draw out any slime.
12. Taste the bhindi fry and, if you wish, add extra salt or a sprinkle of chaat masala for an additional tang.
13. Serve, garnished with fresh coriander if desired.

Notes

a) Hing, also known as asafoetida, is a pungent root used in powdered form in Indian cooking. When raw it has an acrid, unpleasant aroma (it has been nicknamed 'devil's dung'), but when fried in oil it produces a piquant flavour not dissimilar to onion and garlic. It's especially popular in Brahmin and Jain communities in India, which for religious or ethnic reasons eat neither garlic nor onions. On a practical level it can help reduce flatulence – another good reason to try this recipe!
b) You can purchase both hing and amchoor in South Asian stores and of course from online retailers.

Restaurant Style Curries

Coriander & Lemon Achari Mirch

A medium hot, tangy and fresh-tasting curry with lots of fresh coriander and lemon juice, a dash of cream, sugar, and spicy chilli pickle. This curry works nicely with chicken tikka as the main ingredient. Feel free to add vegetables to bulk the sauce out (and to further elongate the name of the dish!).

I thought up this recipe when faced with some leftover ingredients after a curry cooking session. Thrown together as an experiment, I remembered to write the recipe down in detail before forgetting. That is fortunate, because since publishing my recipe (with an accompanying YouTube video) I've had my experiences affirmed on several occasions. I can confirm that, not only is it very popular with both ladies and gentlemen, but it has also been used to rectify several marital misdemeanours!

Ingredients

- 3 TBSP (45 ml) Oil
- 2 tsp Ginger/Garlic paste
- ½-1 tsp Kasuri Methi
- 2 tsp Mix Powder
- ¼ tsp Salt
- ¼ tsp Garam Masala
- ¼ tsp Chilli Powder (optional)
- 300-330ml+ Base Gravy, heated up
- 5 TBSP fresh Coriander Stalks, very finely chopped or blended
- Pre-cooked Chicken, Tikka, Lamb, Vegetables, Prawns, etc.
- 2 TBSP (30ml) Single Cream
- 5 TBSP fresh Coriander Leaves, finely chopped
- 1 TBSP Jaggery or Brown Sugar
- 1 TBSP (15ml) fresh Lemon Juice
- 1–3 tsp Chilli Pickle (optional - adjust to taste)
- ½ a Lemon Slice for garnishing

Method

1. Add the oil to a frying pan on medium high heat.
2. When the oil has heated up, add the ginger/garlic paste. Fry for 20–30 seconds, stirring frequently. Do not let the paste stick to the pan and burn.
3. Add the kasuri methi, mix powder, salt, garam masala, and the optional chilli powder. Continue to fry, stirring frequently for 20-30 seconds, adding a small splash of base gravy to help prevent the spices from burning.
4. Now add the fresh coriander stalks and the main ingredient, e.g. chicken, lamb, chicken tikka, vegetables, etc. If using prawns, add 2-3 minutes before the end of cooking the curry.
5. Turn the heat up to high and add 75ml of base gravy. Stir together, then leave to cook until the sauce has reduced slightly, small craters form around the edges, and there is a visible presence of oil on the surface.
6. Pour in a second 75ml of base gravy, again stirring and scraping the bottom and sides of the pan once when first added and allow the sauce to cook as before.
7. Add 150ml of base gravy, the jaggery/sugar, the fresh lemon juice, and the optional chilli pickle. Mix well.

8. Leave to cook for 3-4 minutes. Avoid stirring or scraping the pan unless you think the curry will soon start to burn. Be brave and see how long your nerve lasts – you may be surprised at the outcome. It takes practice and patience to master the caramelisation technique.
9. Add extra base gravy to thin the sauce out, as desired. You will probably find the need to add at least 100ml extra if you want a medium consistency, considering this curry is not bulked out by tomato paste, chopped onions, or the like.
10. About 1 minute before the anticipated end of cooking, turn down the heat to low, and add the fresh coriander leaves and stir in the single cream. Taste, and if desired, add extra lemon juice, salt, pickle, cream, and/or sugar.
11. Serve, adding a sprinkle of fresh coriander and half a lemon slice on top.

Notes

a) Some brands of chilli pickle are much hotter than others (for example Mr Naga), so be careful. If you prefer less or no chilli heat to this curry, reduce the amount or omit.

Chicken Tikka Coriander & Lemon Achari Mirch

Methi Chicken

The distinctive flavour and aroma of fenugreek (methi) make this curry stand out from the crowd. Both the leaf (ideally fresh, not dried) and seeds are used in this recipe. The whole and crushed spices added at the beginning provide an earthy foundation for the fresh ingredients added later. The addition of tangy and fresh yoghurt augments the slight bitterness of fenugreek.

You can substitute chicken with lamb or vegetables in this recipe if you want to, but I think it works best with poultry.

Ingredients

- 3–4 TBSP (45–60ml) Oil
- ½ tsp Cumin Seeds
- ½ tsp Coriander Seeds (crushed)
- ¼ tsp Fenugreek Seeds
- 1 Star Anise
- 1 Large Asian Bay Leaf, Tej Patta (optional)
- ½ tsp Fennel Seeds (optional)
- 75g Onion, finely chopped
- 1½ tsp Ginger/Garlic Paste
- 1 tsp Mix Powder
- ¼-½ tsp Salt
- ¼-½ tsp Chilli Powder (optional)
- 3-4 TBSP Fenugreek Leaves (Methi), fresh and finely chopped
- 3 TBSP Tomato Paste
- 1 TBSP each of fresh Coriander Stalks and Leaves, finely chopped
- Pre-cooked Chicken
- 330ml+ Base Gravy, heated up
- 2 TBSP Natural Yoghurt

Method

1. Crush the coriander seeds into small pieces with a rolling pin or pestle & mortar.
2. Heat a frying pan on medium high and add the oil.
3. Add the cumin seeds, crushed coriander seeds, fenugreek seeds, star anise, and the optional Asian bay leaf. Cook for 30-40 seconds to infuse flavour into the oil, stirring frequently.
4. Throw in the onion and fry for a couple of minutes until it begins to brown around the edges. Stir occasionally.
5. Add the ginger/garlic paste and continue to cook for 20-30 seconds or until the sizzling subsides and small crackles can be heard. Stir frequently.
6. Next add the mix powder, salt, and the optional chilli powder.
7. Fry for 20-30 seconds, stirring diligently. If the mixture dries out add a splash of base gravy (e.g. 30ml) to avoid burning the spices and give them enough time to cook properly.
8. Add the tomato paste and the fresh fenugreek leaves. Turn up the heat to high, mix together, and then fry until the oil separates and tiny craters appear around the edges of the frying pan.
9. Then add the coriander stalks and the pre-cooked chicken. Coat the meat with the sauce.
10. Add 75ml of base gravy and stir into the sauce. Leave to cook on high heat with no further stirring until the sauce has reduced a little, and craters form again around the edges.

Methi Chicken

11. Next add a second 75ml of base gravy, stir and scrape the bottom and sides of the pan once when first added, and allow the sauce to reduce once again.
12. Then it's in with the final 150ml of base gravy. Stir and scrape the pan initially, and then leave to cook on high heat for 4-5 minutes, or until the desired consistency (medium thick) is reached.
13. During that time, stir and scrape once or twice to mix the caramelised sauce back in, but do this only to prevent the sauce from sticking too much and burning. It's important to let the sauce thicken and caramelise on the bottom and sides of the pan: that produces a fantastic flavour. Add extra base gravy if the sauce is becoming too thick.
14. A minute or two before the end of cooking, turn the heat to low temporarily and add the natural yoghurt and fresh coriander.
15. Retrieve and discard the Asian bay leaf and star anise.
16. Garnish with a few fenugreek leaves and serve.

Notes

a) If you cannot find fresh fenugreek you can use 2½ tsp kasuri methi instead, but you won't get the superior fresh flavour.

Achari Lamb

Lamb has a subtle sweet character that marries well with tart-tasting things. Achari means 'pickled' in Hindi, and achari lamb is a classic curry that melds sweet and tart components magnificently for a festival of flavour in the mouth. You may have also heard of it being called 'achari gosht'.

My BIR version is a medium hot, savoury, piquant curry made with Indian pickle and optional potato chunks. The texture and slight sweetness of the potato works very well with lamb and the tart pickle flavours. It's also a good way to bulk a curry out to go further, so you can expect this to feed up to two people if you use the extra potato chunks.

You can of course use a different main ingredient in an achari curry if you wish. It will still taste great, but in my opinion lamb is the superior option.

Ingredients

- 3-4 TBSP (45-60ml) Oil
- 1 tsp Mustard Seeds
- ¼ tsp Fenugreek Seeds
- ½ tsp Black Cumin Seeds (see Notes)
- ½ tsp Kalonji seeds (aka Nigella Seeds)
- 75-100g Onion, sliced into thin semi-circular rings (approx. half a medium-sized onion)
- 1½ tsp Ginger/Garlic Paste
- 1 tsp Kasuri Methi
- 1½ tsp Kashmiri Chilli Powder or ¾ tsp 'regular' variety
- 1½ tsp Mix Powder
- ¼ tsp Salt
- 5 TBSP Tomato Paste
- 1 TBSP each of fresh Coriander Stalks and Leaves, finely chopped
- 330ml+ Base Gravy, heated up
- Pre-cooked Lamb
- 75g Pre-cooked Potato chunks, about 5 or 6 in number (optional, see Notes)
- 1–1½ TBSP Indian Pickle, for example Mixed, Mango, Lime, Brinjal, Chilli, or Garlic (see Notes)
- 3 TBSP (45ml) Natural Yoghurt
- 3-4 Segments of fresh Tomato

Method

1. Add the oil to a frying pan on medium high heat.
2. Throw in the mustard seeds, fenugreek seeds, black cumin seeds and kalonji seeds. Stir and cook for 30 seconds or until the mustard seeds start popping.
3. Next add the onion slices and cook for 1-2 minutes stirring frequently, until they soften and turn translucent.
4. Now add the ginger/garlic paste and fry for 15-30 seconds until the sound of the sizzling turns to a light crackling.
5. Add the kasuri methi, mix powder, chilli powder, and salt.
6. Fry for 20-30 seconds initially, adding 30ml base gravy to help prevent burning. Stir diligently.
7. Now in with the tomato paste. Turn up the heat to high while stirring constantly until the oil separates and tiny craters appear around the edges of the pan.
8. Then add the pre-cooked lamb and coriander stalks. Mix well into the sauce.
9. Stir in 75ml of base gravy then leave to cook on high heat until the sauce has reduced a little and the craters form again.
10. Now stir in a second 75ml of base gravy and leave to cook again as in the previous step.
11. Pour in 150ml of base gravy, the Indian pickle of your choice, and the pre-cooked potatoes (if you are using them). Stir and scrape the bottom and sides of the pan to mix all the thick bits back into the sauce.

12. Leave to cook on high heat for 3-4 minutes, or until the curry has a nice medium-thick consistency. Add a little extra base gravy to thin the sauce out if desired. Avoid stirring or scraping unless the curry is showing signs of imminently burning.
13. Add the fresh coriander leaves and fresh tomato segments.
14. Turn the heat down and add the natural yoghurt. Stir in and leave to cook for a further 1–2 minutes.
15. Give the curry a taste, and adjust with extra pickle, salt or sugar as desired.
16. Spoon off excess oil from the top of the curry if you want to be health conscious.
17. Garnish with more fresh coriander and an extra tomato segment.

Notes

a) To make life easier, you can use 2½ tsp of panch phoran instead of all the other spice seeds added at the start for a close approximation.

b) There are many types and brands of Indian-style pickles. For a mild but tasty one I suggest brinjal (aubergine) pickle, or for a fruity hot tang, try mango, lime, or satkora (Bengali lime) pickle. For a more aromatic flavour use garlic pickle, or for extreme heat use a naga pickle (use with caution). You can experiment with combinations for added layers of flavour. Mixed pickle varieties are commonly available to buy.

c) Pickles can be salty, so I have reduced the amount of salt added to compensate. You may want to add a little extra after tasting.

d) The pre-cooked potatoes can be made simply by peeling and chunking potato, then simmering in water for 15 minutes with a pinch of salt and turmeric, until they are cooked but still firm.

e) I have tweaked the recipe from that shown in the accompanying YouTube video. Pre-cooked potatoes have been added as an option, the mix powder is reduced from 2 to 1½ tsp, and the onions are now cooked for 1-2 minutes instead of 45-60 seconds.

King Prawn Zafrani

Zafrani is a mild, delicate, aromatic curry infused with saffron, cardamom and fennel, in a sauce with added tamarind, cream, and fresh coriander. I find this curry works very well with king prawns, which are added near the end of the curry cooking. Alternatively, pre-cooked chicken or chicken tikka also perform admirably in a zafrani curry.

Saffron is a spice created from the strands within the crocus flower. It's the world's most expensive spice when measured by weight, mostly because it needs to be harvested by hand. It has a very special, clean, delicate, yet pronounced flavour that will please your taste buds.

Ingredients

- A small pinch of Saffron (12-15 strands)
- 3 TBSP (45ml) Oil, Ghee or a combination
- 10cm Cassia Bark or Cinnamon Stick
- 1 tsp Fennel Seeds
- 100g Onion, sliced
- 1½-2 tsp Ginger/Garlic Paste
- 1tsp Kasuri Methi
- 1¼ tsp Mix Powder
- ½ tsp Tandoori Masala
- ¼ tsp Salt, to taste
- ½ tsp Kashmiri Chilli Powder (optional)
- 4 TBSP Tomato Paste
- 1½ TBSP each of fresh Coriander Stalks and Leaves, finely chopped
- 1 tsp Elachi Powder or the seeds from 3-4 Green Cardamom Pods
- Pre-cooked Chicken or Chicken Tikka (if using meat instead of prawns)
- 330ml+ Base Gravy, heated up
- 1 TBSP Tamarind Table Sauce, ½ tsp Tamarind Concentrate, or 2-3 tsp Tamarind Pulp
- 150-175g King Prawns, raw (translucent) or pre-cooked (pink) - if using prawns
- 3 TBSP (45ml) Single Cream
- A Sprinkle of Saffron to garnish
- A Wedge of Lemon or Lime

Method

1. Soak the saffron strands with a little hot water (or milk) in a small cup and set aside.
2. Add the oil to a frying pan on medium high heat.
3. Throw in the cassia bark and fennel seeds.
4. Fry for 30-45 seconds to infuse the oil while stirring frequently.
5. Now add the onion slices and cook for 2-3 minutes until soft and browned very slightly.
6. Next add the ginger/garlic paste. Fry for 30-40 seconds or until it just starts to brown and the sizzling sound lessens. Stir frequently to stop it sticking to the pan.
7. Add the kasuri methi, mix powder, tandoori masala, salt, and the optional Kashmiri chilli powder.
8. Fry for 20-30 seconds, stirring very frequently. Add a little base gravy (e.g. 30ml) if the mixture dries out and sticks to the pan. This avoids burning the spices and gives them enough time to cook properly.
9. Add the tomato paste, coriander stalks, elachi powder or green cardamom seeds, and turn up the heat to high.
10. If using pre-cooked chicken, tikka, lamb, or other pre-cooked meat, add it now and mix well, making sure the meat pieces are coated in the sauce.
11. Add 75ml of base gravy, mix, then leave to cook for 30-45 seconds with no further stirring.
12. Then add a second 75ml of base gravy, stir into the sauce, and leave on high heat with no further stirring until the sauce is reduced a little, and small, dry craters form around the edges.

13. Stir in a final 150ml of base gravy and the tamarind.
14. Leave to cook on high heat for 3-4 minutes. Stir and scrape once or twice to mix the caramelised sauce back in, but do this only to prevent the sauce from sticking too much and burning. Do however let the sauce thicken and caramelise on the bottom and sides of the pan - this gives a superb flavour.
15. Now add the king prawns and the saffron water. Bear in mind that they will release a little water when cooking which will thin the sauce out a bit.
16. Reduce the heat to low and pour in the single cream and add the fresh coriander leaves.
17. Cook for a further 2-2½ minutes or until the prawns have heated through and are thoroughly cooked. Add some extra base gravy near the end of cooking if it appears to be thickening up too much.
18. Taste and season with salt and/or mango chutney to taste.
19. Fish out the cassia bark and discard it. You can also spoon off any excess oil from the surface of the curry if you wish.
20. Serve garnished with a wedge of lemon/lime and a sprinkle of saffron strands.

Notes

a) Saffron can be bought in small plastic boxes at reasonable prices from many South Asian food shops and supermarkets. It's used sparingly so does go a long way.
b) Raw prawns are best for this curry, either fresh or defrosted from frozen. Pre-cooked prawns are OK but can turn rubbery easily.
c) You can of course use small prawns instead of the larger variety. Care should be taken not to overcook them.
d) I have reduced the amount of cream in this recipe to 45ml from the 75ml that is captioned in the accompanying YouTube video. I have also increased the fennel seeds from ½ to 1 tsp and reduced the amount of salt to ¼ tsp to compensate for the saltiness of the prawns.

Kalimirch

Black pepper (Hindi: kali mirch) ceases to be the understudy and comes forward to play the lead role in this pungent medium strength curry featuring a creamy sauce balanced with lemon juice and chef's 'special herbs and spices'.

This curry works well with chicken. Make it with cauliflower instead for a delicious vegetarian alternative.

Ingredients

- 3 TBSP Oil (45ml)
- 1½-2 tsp Black Peppercorns, toasted and coarsely crushed
- ½ tsp Cumin Seeds
- ½ tsp Fennel Seeds (optional)
- 75g–100g Onion, very finely chopped
- 1½ tsp Ginger/Garlic Paste
- 1 tsp Kasuri Methi
- 1¼ tsp Mix Powder
- ¼-½ tsp Salt
- Pinch of Garam Masala (about one eighth of a tsp)
- ½ tsp Kashmiri Chilli Powder (or regular, optional)
- 330ml+ Base Gravy, heated up
- 1½-2 TBSP Tomato Paste
- Pre-cooked Chicken, Lamb, Tikka, Vegetables, etc.
- 1 tsp Lemon Juice
- 1 tsp Sugar
- 3-4 splashes of Worcestershire Sauce (optional)
- 4 TBSP (60ml) Single Cream
- Finely sliced Ginger juliennes for garnishing
- Black Pepper powder for garnishing (freshly ground is best)
- Fresh Coriander Leaves for garnishing

Method

1. Add the whole black peppercorns to a dry frying pan on medium heat. Toast them gently for 1 minute to enhance the flavour. Gently shake the pan a few times to prevent burning.
2. Then coarsely grind them with a pestle & mortar or a spice/coffee grinder.
3. Add the oil to a frying pan and heat up to medium high.
4. Throw the crushed black peppercorns in along with the cumin seeds and the optional fennel seeds. Fry for 30-40 seconds to infuse flavour into the oil, stirring frequently.
5. Now add the chopped onion. Fry for about 1–2 minutes until the onion begins to soften and turn translucent. Stir from time to time to avoid burning.
6. Add the ginger/garlic paste and continue to cook for 20-30 seconds or until the sizzling starts turning into a subtle crackling sound. Stir diligently.
7. Next add the kasuri methi, mix powder, salt, garam masala, and the optional chilli powder.
8. Fry for 20-30 seconds, stirring very frequently. If the mixture dries out and sticks to the pan add a little base gravy (e.g. 30ml) to avoid burning the spices and to give them enough time to cook properly.

Chicken Kalimirch

9. Add the tomato paste and your choice of pre-cooked meat or vegetables. Turn up the heat to high and mix well.
10. Add 75ml of base gravy, stir into the sauce, and leave on high heat with no further stirring until the sauce is reduced a little, tiny craters form around the edges, and there is visible separation of oil.
11. Next add a second 75ml of base gravy, stirring and scraping the bottom and sides of the pan once when first added, allowing the sauce to reduce again.
12. Then add 150ml of base gravy, the lemon juice, sugar, and optional Worcestershire sauce.
13. Stir and scrape the pan then leave to cook on high heat for 4-5 minutes. Stir and scrape once or twice to mix the caramelised sauce back in, but do this only to prevent the sauce from sticking too much and burning. It's important to let the sauce adhere to the bottom and sides of the pan, which produces a great flavour.
14. A minute or so before the anticipated end of cooking, turn the heat down to low and add the single cream. Stir in, taste, and season with extra salt, sugar, lemon juice, and/or black pepper if desired.
15. Aim to get a medium thickness with a smooth sauce. Add more base gravy if needed.
16. Garnish with ginger juliennes, freshly ground black pepper, and finely chopped fresh coriander.

Shimla Mirch

Fresh green capsicum features heavily in this medium hot dish, which is served with a topping of raw fresh vegetables and some optional pineapple. The contrasting topping adds a toothsome textural dimension and a welcome refreshing experience for the palate.

Shimla mirch is the Hindi phrase for capsicum or bell pepper, and is named after Shimla, the capital city of the northern Indian state of Himachal Pradesh, which is known for its large-scale cultivation of peppers.

Ingredients

- 3-4 TBSP Oil (45-60ml)
- 100-125g Green Pepper, finely diced
- 70g Onion, finely diced
- 1½ tsp Ginger/Garlic Paste
- 1½ tsp Mix Powder
- ¼ tsp Chilli Powder
- ¼ tsp Salt
- 1 tsp Kasuri Methi
- 3-4 TBSP Tomato Paste
- 330ml+ Base Gravy, heated up
- Pre-cooked Chicken/Lamb/Beef, etc.
- ½ tsp Jaggery or Brown Sugar. 1 tsp White Sugar can be used instead

The Topping:

- 10g Red or regular (Brown) Onion, finely diced (pre-soaked in water to remove some of the harshness. Red onion is milder)
- 1 TBSP fresh Coriander Leaf, finely chopped
- 2-3 tsp fresh Lemon or Lime Juice

- ¼ tsp Garam Masala
- 1 Green Chilli, finely chopped (optional)
- ¼ tsp Chaat Masala (optional)
- 1 tsp fresh Ginger, finely sliced into strips (optional)
- 25g Pineapple (a few chunks), chopped small (optional)

Method

1. Start by mixing the topping ingredients together in a bowl and set aside. Beforehand, soak the onion for the topping in cold water with a dash of lemon juice for 15 minutes to remove some of the harshness if desired.
2. Add the oil to a frying pan on medium high heat.
3. Next add the diced green pepper and onion. Fry for 1½-2½ minutes until softened but not browned, stirring often.
4. Now throw in the ginger/garlic paste, stirring until the sizzling subsides.
5. Add the mix powder, chilli powder, salt, kasuri methi, and a small amount of base gravy (e.g. 30ml) to help the spices fry without burning.
6. Fry for 20-30 seconds, stirring frequently.
7. Add the tomato paste, turn the heat up to high, and fry 30 seconds or until the oil separates and small dry craters appear around the edges of the pan.
8. Add the pre-cooked chicken/lamb/beef and mix well into the sauce.
9. Now add the first 75ml of base gravy, stir into the sauce, and leave on high heat (not stirring) until the sauce has reduced slightly and the dry craters form again.
10. Add a second 75ml of base gravy, stir and scrape the bottom and sides of the

pan once when first added, and leave the sauce to reduce again.
11. Next add the sugar and the final 150ml of base gravy. Stir and stir/scrape once when first added.
12. Leave to cook on high heat for 4-5 minutes. Don't stir/scrape unless the curry shows signs of imminently starting to burn.
13. Near the end of cooking add a little extra base gravy if desired to thin the sauce out as to your preference.
14. Sprinkle the mixed topping ingredients on to the curry.
15. Taste and sprinkle on a little extra salt or chaat masala if desired.
16. Garnish with extra some green pepper and serve.

Notes

a) The recipe differs slightly from the accompanying YouTube video. I have increased the amount of green pepper, halved the overly generous topping, included optional chaat masala, and fine-tuned some of the timings very slightly.

Chicken Shimla Mirch

Pudina

A smooth, refreshing yet indulgent curry featuring the heavy use of fresh mint (Hindi: pudina). Complementary flavours such as chilli, coriander and lemon juice bring out the minty freshness. A touch of cream or yoghurt adds a little rich roundness, and a squeeze of runny honey added at the end transports this dish into another dimension.

Mint marries with lamb harmoniously so I recommended that combination, but you could try it with chicken or vegetables instead.

Ingredients

- 3 TBSP (45ml) Oil
- 1½ tsp Panch Phoran (see Notes)
- 75g Onion, cut into semi-circular slices
- 2 tsp Ginger/Garlic Paste
- 1 tsp Kasuri Methi
- 1¼ tsp Mix Powder
- ¼ tsp Chilli Powder (optional)
- ¼-½ tsp Salt
- 150-200g Pre-cooked Lamb, Chicken, Vegetables, etc.
- 330ml+ Base Gravy, heated up
- Pudina Paste (see right)
- 1 TBSP Lamb Stock (optional, see Notes)
- 2 TBSP Single Cream or Full Fat Yoghurt
- Pinch of Garam Masala
- 1-1½ TBSP Honey (see Notes)
- 1 Cucumber Slice and few extra Mint Leaves to garnish

Pudina Paste

Chop and blend these ingredients into a smooth paste:

4 TBSP fresh Mint Leaves
1½ TBSP fresh Coriander Stalks
½ fresh Green Chilli
½-1 Garlic Clove
1-1½ tsp Mint Sauce (from a jar)
1 tsp Lemon Juice
A splash of Water to help blending

Lamb Pudina

Restaurant Style Curries

Method

1. Prepare the pudina paste (see opposite page) and set aside.
2. Add the oil to a frying pan on medium high heat.
3. When the oil is hot, add the panch phoran and fry until the black mustard seeds start to pop.
4. Add the onion slices. Fry for 1-2 minutes until softened, then add the ginger/garlic paste. Fry until just starting to brown and the sizzling sound reduces, whilst stirring diligently. Don't let it stick to the pan and burn.
5. Next add the kasuri methi, mix powder, salt, and the optional chilli powder.
6. Fry for 20-30 seconds, stirring very frequently. If the mixture dries out and sticks to the pan, add a little base gravy (30ml) to avoid burning the spices and give them enough time to cook properly.
7. Turn up the heat to high, and mix in the pre-cooked lamb, chicken, etc.
8. Now add 75ml of base gravy. Mix and let cook for 30-45 seconds with no further stirring.
9. Then add a second 75ml of base gravy, stir into the sauce, and leave on high heat with no further stirring until the sauce is reduced a little, and small, dry craters form around the edges.
10. Stir in the pudina paste, 150ml of base gravy, and the optional lamb stock.
11. Leave to cook on high heat for 3-4 minutes. Stir and scrape once or twice to mix the caramelised sauce back in, but do this only to prevent the sauce from sticking too much and burning. It's important to let the sauce adhere to the bottom and sides of the pan, which produces a great flavour.
12. Turn the heat to low, and stir in the cream or yoghurt, and a pinch of garam masala.
13. Cook for a further minute, adding some extra base gravy near the end of cooking if it appears to be thickening up too much.
14. Mix in the honey just before the end.
15. Taste and add extra mint sauce, honey, lemon juice and/or salt if desired.
16. Serve garnished with a few fresh mint leaves and a slice of cucumber.

Notes

a) Panch phoran (spelling varies) is a whole seed mixture of fenugreek, fennel, cumin, kalonji (nigella), and black mustard seeds. It can be purchased ready assembled from South Asian food shops and supermarkets.

b) Adding lamb stock to this dish (or indeed any meat-based curry) enhances the flavour nicely. Be mindful of how salty the stock is and adjust the salt accordingly when adding it with the spices.

c) This recipe has been adjusted slightly from the corresponding YouTube video. I have removed the sugar from the paste, and now at the end of cooking add honey which works incredibly well with mint.

Chicken Tikka Kashmir

Kashmir

Those of you who have read Indian Restaurant Curry at Home Volume 1 may well know that I'm not normally a fan of sweet BIR curries such as the korma. Well that changes right here with this recipe – one could describe it as korma's older and wiser sibling.

My version of a BIR Kashmir curry (sometimes listed on the menu as 'Bangalore') is indeed sweet, but its complex layers of flavour paint a beautiful picture. As with some other rich Northern sub-continent curries such as moghul and pasanda, it has a profusion of nuts, cream, and fruit. As you will notice in the list of ingredients, banana is used generously, and tamarind, yoghurt, and Kashmiri chilli powder provide hints of sourness and heat.

Ingredients

- 2-3 TBSP (30-45ml) Oil, Ghee, or a combination of the two
- 10cm Cassia Bark
- 3 Green Cardamom Pods, split open
- 2 Cloves
- 35g Yellow or Red Pepper, cut into ½ cm wide strips (about one sixth of a medium sized pepper)
- 1 tsp Kashmiri Chilli Powder (optional)
- 1 tsp Mix Powder
- ¼ tsp Turmeric
- ¼ tsp Salt
- ¼ tsp Garam Masala
- Pre-cooked Chicken, Lamb, Vegetables, etc.
- 330ml+ Base Gravy, heated up
- 3 TBSP Almond Powder
- ¾ tsp fresh Ginger, peeled and sliced into very fine strips
- 2 tsp Tamarind Sauce or ½-1 tsp Tamarind Concentrate, or 2 tsp fresh Lemon or Lime Juice
- 1 TBSP Mango Chutney
- 1 TBSP Sugar
- 3 TBSP Natural Yoghurt
- 100-120g Banana, sliced thickly
- 1 TBSP Almond Flakes, toasted
- 1-2 TBSP (15-30ml) Single Cream for garnishing

Method

1. In a dry frying pan toast the almond flakes on low-medium heat for 1-2 minutes. Flip them over from time to time to brown then evenly. Remove from the pan and set aside.
2. Add the oil/ghee to the same frying pan on medium high heat.
3. Now add the cassia bark, green cardamom, cloves, and the pepper. Cook for 30 seconds, stirring frequently.
4. Then add the mix powder, turmeric, salt, garam masala, and the optional Kashmiri chilli powder.
5. Fry for 20-30 seconds, stirring diligently. Add a splash of base gravy to help prevent burning and to give enough time for the spices to cook properly.
6. Next add the pre-cooked chicken, lamb, tikka, vegetables etc., and mix well into the sauce.
7. Add the almond powder and 150ml of base gravy and mix well into the sauce.
8. Turn up the heat to high and leave to cook for 1-2 minutes to reduce the sauce and to allow the base gravy to stick to the pan and caramelise a little.
9. Now add a second 150ml of base gravy, fresh ginger, tamarind or lemon juice, mango chutney, sugar, and natural yoghurt.

10. Mix together well, scraping the caramelised bits from the bottom and sides of the frying pan.
11. Reduce the heat to medium and let cook for 3-4 minutes, or until the desired consistency (quite thick) is reached. Make sure the almond powder has dissolved into the sauce and is not overly grainy.
12. Add the banana slices a couple of minutes before the end of cooking.
13. Avoid stirring and do so only to prevent the sauce sticking to the pan too much and burning. Add extra base gravy if desired during cooking to thin the sauce out.
14. Remove the whole spices, sprinkle a small pinch of garam masala on top and stir once.
15. Serve, scattering the toasted almond flakes and drizzling the single cream on top.

Notes

a) If the banana is firm and unripe it's best to add the slices with the second 150ml of base gravy to give it time to cook and soften up.
b) The tamarind is for sourness, flavour, and as a 'tip of the hat' to authentic Kashmiri cuisine. Other authentic ingredients include the Kashmiri chilli powder, yoghurt, almond, fresh ginger, green cardamom, cassia and cloves.
c) The banana, while not wholly authentic, gives this curry some extra texture and flavour, and is quite common in curries of the same or similar name in British Indian Restaurants and takeaways.
d) I've increased the amount of banana in this recipe from 60g to 100-120g as compared to the corresponding YouTube video. Misty Ricardo likes bananas!

Chicken Moghul

Moghul

The Persian-influenced cuisine of the Mughals is traditionally rich and extravagant, often including cream, fruit, and nuts. The Mughal Empire spanned most of the Indian subcontinent dating back from the 16th to the early-mid 18th century. They fused Persian and Indian traditions and left a special imprint on the multi-faceted tapestry of Indian cuisine.

Unsurprisingly, when you order a moghul curry in a restaurant you would be right to expect a creamy, sweet, and deliciously decadent dish.

This is my version, and while it bears a similarity to the pasanda curry there are some key differences that set it apart. It's a rich, nutty, creamy-based curry of mild-medium heat. A touch of sugar adds a little sweetness, and the curry is enhanced further by specially selected spices and other ingredients, not least being the optional hard-boiled egg. Works well with chicken or lamb.

Ingredients

- 3 TBSP Oil, Ghee, or a combination
- 8cm Cassia Bark
- 2 Cloves
- 2 Green Cardamom (split open or just use the seeds from within)
- 70g Red Pepper, finely diced
- 1½ tsp Garlic, very finely chopped
- 1 tsp Ginger, very finely chopped
- 1 tsp Kasuri Methi
- 1 tsp Mix Powder
- ¼ tsp Turmeric
- ¼-½ tsp Chilli Powder
- ¼-½ tsp Salt
- 300ml+ Base Gravy, heated up
- 3 TBSP Almond Powder
- 2-3 tsp White Sugar
- Pre-cooked Chicken or Lamb
- 2-3 tsp Onion Paste (aka Bunjarra. Optional)
- A few splashes of Worcestershire Sauce (optional)
- 1 tsp Lemon or Lime Juice
- 10-15 Sultanas (optional)
- 100-125ml Single Cream, plus a little extra for garnishing
- 1-2 tsp Butter Ghee (optional)
- A small pinch of Garam Masala
- Fresh Coriander for garnishing, finely chopped
- Half a Hard-Boiled Egg (optional, see Notes section)

Method

1. Add the oil/ghee to a frying pan on medium high heat.
2. Add the cassia bark, cloves, and green cardamom. Fry for 45-60 seconds, stirring to infuse the oil.
3. Then add the red pepper, and fry for 1-2 minutes until soft, stirring occasionally.
4. Next throw in the garlic and ginger and continue frying for 30 seconds.
5. Add the kasuri methi, mix powder, turmeric, salt, almond powder, white sugar, and the optional chilli powder.
6. Fry for 20-30 seconds, initially adding 75ml base gravy to help prevent burning. Stir diligently.
7. Now add the pre-cooked chicken or lamb, mix well, and turn up the heat to high.

8. Add 225ml base gravy, lemon juice, and the optional onion paste and Worcestershire sauce.
9. Stir and scrape the contents of the pan together then leave to cook on high heat for 3-4 minutes. Resist the urge to meddle while cooking so that the curry can caramelise and develop flavour. It may need stirring once or twice to avoid burning, but do this only when necessary.
10. About 1-2 minutes before the end of cooking, turn the heat down to low then add the single cream and the optional sultanas. Return the heat to high once mixed in.
11. Feel free to add extra base gravy near the end of cooking to give the curry more volume.
12. Taste the sauce, and if desired add more salt, sugar, or cream.
13. If you want extra richness and a nice sheen, you can add 1-2 tsp of butter ghee just before serving. However, if you are being health conscious, then spoon any surplus oil from the top of the curry instead.
14. Serve topped with a sprinkle of garam masala, extra cream, and a scattering of fresh coriander. For extra decadence finish it off with half a hard-boiled egg.

Notes

a) I'm not wanting to teach grandma to suck (or boil) eggs here, but to hard-boil one, simmer the egg in plenty of boiling, salted water for 8-10 minutes. Place the hot egg in cold water for a few minutes so it's easy to handle, then gently peel the shell off. For a vibrant and appealing orange colour, fry the egg in a little oil with ½ tsp turmeric on low-medium heat for a minute or two. Keep turning the egg in the pan to get it evenly 'oranged'.

b) The corresponding YouTube video recipe differs from this book's recipe. Here I have made some ingredient changes – chopped ginger instead of juliennes, increased the chilli powder range, removed the black pepper, increased the oil slightly, and introduced fresh coriander to the garnishing. The main reason for the changes was to differentiate the moghul from a pasanda curry.

Chicken Tikka Shashlik

These succulent kebabs are very easy to make once you have some marinated raw chicken tikka to hand. Skewer up the chicken with chunks of onion and pepper, plonk it under the grill or on your barbeque, and before you know it you've got a super delicious feast on a stick. Season the kebabs with lemon juice and chaat masala for an extra twist.

I've included enough in the ingredients to make three large kebabs (as you can see in the photo). That will be easily enough for three people as a starter, probably more. There are so many ways to serve this shashlik. For example, as a simple starter, as a main course alongside rice, salad and raita, chopped up and wrapped in a naan bread, or to impress others, smugly serve it to your special friends and family on a smoking hot cast iron sizzler dish.

Please see my Chicken Tikka recipe on page 21 for how to prepare and marinate the chicken.

Ingredients

- 500-600g Chicken Tikka, marinated and uncooked (see my recipe here)
- 1 medium large Onion, cut into large segments
- ½ a Green Pepper and ½ a Red Pepper, cut into large segments
- A few large Button Mushrooms, halved (optional)
- 4 Garlic Cloves, peeled and minced or chopped very finely
- 1 tsp Kasuri Methi
- ¾ tsp Salt
- 30ml Oil or Butter Ghee
- ½ tsp Chaat Masala
- For garnishing: fresh Coriander Leaves and Red or Brown Onion Slices
- Lemon Wedges to serve on the side

Method

1. Mix together the onion and pepper segments, the mushroom halves (if using), and the garlic, kasuri methi, salt, and oil in a bowl.
2. Assemble the kebabs on metal skewers by sliding on alternate chunks of raw chicken tikka, onion, pepper, and optional mushroom. The metallic property of the skewers will help cook the chicken from the inside.
3. Brush your grill rack with a little oil to stop the kebabs sticking while they are cooking. A layer of aluminium foil underneath in the grill pan will make the unavoidable cleaning easier later.
4. Pre-heat your grill or barbeque to 220-240°C (i.e. high).
5. Put the kebabs evenly spaced onto the grill rack and brush the top with a little oil to help the chicken stay moist.
6. Place under the hot grill for 7-8 minutes or until the kebabs are nicely charred on top.
7. Brush a little oil on top again, then turn them over and brush the turned side.
8. Put back under the grill for another 7-8 minutes.
9. Cut into a large piece of chicken to make sure it is cooked in the middle. There should be no pink or translucent patches. If there are then place back under the grill for a couple of minutes and test again with another large chunk of chicken.
10. Voila! Your next decision will be to decide how to serve it. Whichever way you do, I recommend a good squeeze of fresh lemon juice and a generous sprinkle of chaat masala.

Restaurant Style Curries

Adrak

In my opinion the hearty and fiery ginger root (the Hindi word is 'adrak') merits a specially dedicated curry of its own. My version is a medium-hot curry featuring an abundance of fresh ginger and is complemented with onions, green pepper, tomato, mango chutney, and optional pineapple. Cassia bark, green cardamom, and optional fennel seeds or star anise provide complementary aromatic flavours.

Ingredients

- 4 TBSP Oil (60ml). Use Butter Ghee or Vegetable Ghee instead or in part for a more rounded flavour
- 10cm Cassia Bark
- Seeds from 3 Green Cardamoms. Discard the outer pods
- 1 Star Anise or 1 tsp Fennel Seeds (optional)
- 75g Onion, thickly sliced
- 75g Green Pepper, cut into small triangles (approx. half a medium pepper)
- 1½ tsp Ginger/Garlic Paste
- 1¼ TBSP fresh Ginger, peeled and cut into small ½cm pieces
- 1 tsp Kasuri Methi
- 1¼ tsp Mix Powder
- ¾ tsp Kashmiri Chilli Powder (regular chilli powder may be used instead)
- Pinch of Garam Masala (about one eighth of a tsp)
- ¼-½ tsp Salt
- 330ml+ Base Gravy, heated up
- 5-6 TBSP Tomato Paste
- Pre-cooked Chicken, Lamb, Prawns, Vegetables, etc.
- 1-2 TBSP fresh Coriander Stalks, very finely chopped
- 80g Pineapple Chunks (optional)
- 1¼ tsp Lemon or Lime Juice
- 2-3 tsp Mango Chutney
- Fresh Coriander Leaves for garnishing

Method

1. Add the oil/ghee to a frying pan and heat to medium high.
2. Then add the cassia bark, green cardamom seeds, and the optional star anise or fennel seeds.
3. Cook for 30-40 seconds to infuse flavour into the oil, stirring frequently.
4. Add the onion and green pepper. Fry for about 2 minutes to soften and brown slightly, stirring often.
5. Now add the ginger/garlic paste and most of the finely cubed fresh ginger (save some for garnishing). Continue to fry for 15-30 seconds until the sizzling lessens, stirring frequently.
6. Next, add the kasuri methi, mix powder, garam masala, Kashmiri chilli powder, and salt.
7. Fry for 20-30 seconds, stirring very frequently. Add a little base gravy (e.g. 30ml) if the mixture dries out and sticks to the pan. This avoids burning the spices and gives them enough time to cook properly.
8. Add the tomato paste, the fresh coriander stalks, and your choice of main ingredient. Turn up the heat to high and mix together well.
9. Then stir in 75ml of base gravy and leave on high heat with no further fiddling until the sauce has reduced a little, and small craters form again around the edges.

10. Next add a second 75ml of base gravy, stirring and scraping the bottom and sides of the pan once when first added. Allow the sauce to reduce slightly and for the cratering to form up again.
11. Add 150ml of base gravy, the mango chutney, lemon/lime juice, and the optional pineapple chunks.
12. Stir and scrape the pan and leave to cook on high heat for 4-5 minutes. Stir and scrape once or twice to mix the caramelised sauce back in, but do this only to prevent the sauce from sticking too much and burning. It's important to let the sauce adhere to the bottom and sides of the pan - it produces a great flavour.
13. Add a little extra base gravy if needed to achieve a final consistency of medium thickness.
14. Remove the whole spices from the curry.
15. Taste, and add more salt, lemon, or mango chutney if desired.
16. Serve, garnished with the remaining fresh ginger cubes and some finely chopped fresh coriander.

Chicken Tikka Adrak

Shorshe Masala

This is an unusual curry born out of my experiment using leftovers one day. I tried out the combination of English mustard, cream, and honey, and the outcome was this recipe, which is a medium-hot curry with the punchy piquancy of mustard and Bengali spices balanced harmoniously by honey and a little vinegar. Cream is added to create a smooth rounded flavour through which all the flavours can surface.

I gave this dish its name from the word 'shorshe', the Bengali word for mustard.

Chicken Shorshe Masala

Ingredients

- 3 TBSP Oil (45ml). Optionally use up to 1 TBSP of Mustard Oil as part of the total for extra tang
- 1 tsp Panch Phoran (Bengali 5 spice seed mix)
- 2 Cloves
- ½ tsp Coriander Powder (toasted and freshly ground is best)
- ¼ tsp Black Pepper Powder (toasted and freshly ground is best)
- 1 tsp Mix Powder
- ¼ tsp Salt
- ½ tsp Chilli Powder (optional)
- 4 TBSP Special Mustard Paste (see below)
- Pre-cooked Chicken/Lamb/Vegetables, etc.
- 330ml+ Base Gravy, heated up
- 1½-2 tsp Honey. Jaggery or Brown Sugar can be substituted
- 40ml Single Cream
- Fresh Coriander to garnish

Special Mustard Paste

This makes a bit more than the amount needed (4 TBSP) for this recipe. All the following ingredients are chopped and blended to a paste:

- 2-3 tsp Yellow Mustard Powder or 2-3 tsp ready-made English or Dijon Mustard from a jar
- 1 tsp Kasuri Methi
- ½ tsp Turmeric
- 40g Onion
- 1 TBSP fresh Coriander Stalks
- 2-3 Cloves Garlic
- 2-3 tsp Vinegar (e.g. cider, white wine, malt). If using ready-made mustard, reduce this quantity to 1 tsp as it will most likely contain vinegar already
- 1½ cm chunk of fresh Ginger
- ½ tsp Elachi Powder (cardamom seed powder), or the whole seeds from within the pods. (Optional)
- 2-3 Green Chillis (optional)
- 2 TBSP Water (to help blend)

Method

1. Firstly, toast and grind the coriander seeds and black peppercorns to a powder, and then make the special mustard paste (see above).
2. Add the oil to a frying pan or korai on medium high heat.
3. When hot, add the panch phoran and cloves. Stir until the black mustard seeds within the seed mixture start to pop.
4. Add the coriander and black pepper powders, mix powder, salt, and the optional chilli powder.
5. Fry for 20-30 seconds, stirring diligently. Add a small amount of base gravy (e.g. 30ml) to help the spices fry without burning.
6. Turn the heat up to high and add 4 TBSP of the special mustard paste prepared earlier. Stir and leave to fry for 20-30 seconds.

Restaurant Style Curries

7. Add the pre-cooked chicken/lamb/vegetables, etc., and mix well into the sauce.
8. Now add the first 75ml of base gravy, stir into the sauce, and leave on high heat (not stirring) until the sauce is reduced a bit and tiny craters form near the edges of the pan.
9. Add a second 75ml of base gravy, stirring and scraping the bottom and sides of the pan once when first added, allowing the sauce to reduce once again.
10. Now, add 150ml of base gravy and the honey or sugar. Stir and scrape once when first added.
11. Leave to cook on high heat for 5-6 minutes, or until the desired consistency is reached (medium thickness). Add a bit more base gravy if desired to thin the sauce out. Allow the sauce to stick and thicken on the bottom and sides of the pan - avoid stirring unless you think it might burn.
12. A couple of minutes before the end of cooking, turn the heat down to low temporarily and stir in the single cream. Taste, and add extra salt, mustard and/or honey/sugar if desired.
13. Locate and remove the two cloves. They should be easy to spot as the curry is quite light in colour.
14. If you are calorie-conscious spoon off excess oil from the top of the curry.
15. Serve, sprinkling fresh coriander on top.

Notes

a) Varieties of ready-made mustard differ greatly in strength. Go easy on how much you add to the paste. You can always compensate with extra later when tasting.

b) There are two slight adaptations from the corresponding YouTube video recipe – the option of using some mustard oil, base gravy increased from 280ml to 330ml+, and the amount of mustard powder decreased from 1¼ TBSP to 2-3 tsp.

Lamb Chana Saagwala

Lamb chana saagwala is a mild-medium, fresh tasting curry featuring spinach, chickpeas (chana), and a hint of mint. This curry is made for lamb or mutton, but the meat can be omitted for a very tasty vegetarian/vegan dish.

This Misty Ricardo recipe yields a portion larger than my usual curry portion size and should be just enough to feed two people, alongside rice or naan.

Ingredients

- 3 TBSP (45ml Oil)
- 10cm Cassia Bark
- 2-3 Green Cardamom Pods, split open
- ½ tsp Cumin Seeds
- 1 tsp Mustard Seeds
- 80g Onion, cut thinly into semi-circular or quarter-circle slices
- 1–2 tsp Ginger/Garlic Paste
- 1 tsp Kasuri Methi
- 1½ tsp Mix Powder
- ¼ tsp Garam Masala
- ½-1 tsp Kashmiri Chilli Powder (optional)
- ½ tsp Salt
- 330ml+ Base Gravy, heated up
- 4 TBSP Tomato Paste
- 80-100g Chickpeas, pre-cooked (see Notes)
- Pre-cooked Lamb/Mutton
- 2-3 tsp Onion Paste (optional)
- 2-3 tsp Lamb Stock (optional)
- A few of splashes of Worcestershire Sauce (optional)
- 140g Wilted Spinach (weight after squeezing water out), chopped. A 250g packet of fresh spinach yields just the right amount
- 1-2 tsp Mint Sauce or 1 tsp Dried Mint
- 1 tsp Lemon Juice
- 2 fresh Tomato Quarters
- 1-2 tsp Butter Ghee or Butter (optional)
- 1 TBSP fresh Coriander, finely chopped (for garnishing)

Method

1. Add the oil to a frying pan or korai on medium high heat.
2. Throw in the cassia bark, green cardamom, cumin seeds and mustard seeds. Stir diligently for 45-60 seconds to infuse the oil with flavour, or until the mustard seeds start popping.
3. Next, add the onion. Fry for 1½-2 minutes until softened, but not browned. Stir often.
4. Now add the ginger/garlic paste and cook for 30-40 seconds whilst stirring, until sizzling sound lessens.
5. Add the kasuri methi, mix powder, garam masala, salt, the optional Kashmiri chilli powder, and a small amount of base gravy (e.g. 30ml) to help the spices fry without burning.
6. Fry for 20-30 seconds, stirring constantly.
7. Pour in the tomato paste. Turn up the heat to high while stirring frequently for 30 seconds, or until the oil separates and tiny craters appear.
8. Add the chickpeas and the pre-cooked lamb/mutton. Mix well into the sauce.
9. Now add the first 75ml of base gravy, stir into the sauce, and leave on high heat (without further stirring) until the sauce is reduced a little and the craters form again.

Lamb Chana Sagwala

10. Add a second 75ml of base gravy, stirring and scraping the bottom and sides of the pan once when first added, allowing the sauce to reduce once again.
11. Add the optional onion paste, lamb stock, and/or Worcestershire sauce.
12. Next add the spinach, mint, lemon juice, and the final 150ml of base gravy. Stir and scrape once when first added.
13. Leave to cook on high heat for 4-6 minutes. Avoid stirring/scraping unless the curry shows signs of imminently starting to burn, so allowing the sauce to caramelise on the bottom and sides of the pan.
14. If desired, add a little extra base gravy to thin the sauce out.
15. Add the fresh tomato a couple of minutes before the anticipated end of cooking.
16. Taste and add a little sugar, or extra salt, mint, and/or lemon juice if desired.
17. Locate and remove the whole spices then add a knob of butter ghee or regular butter (optional).
18. Spoon off excess oil from the top of the curry if you want to be health conscious.
19. Serve garnished with fresh coriander.

Notes

a) If you are starting off with dry chickpeas you must first soak them overnight in plenty of water and then simmer them for 1-1½ hours, or until tender.
b) The recipe for the optional onion paste and lamb stock can be found in Volume 1.
c) If you're making a vegetarian/vegan version of this dish and you want to include Worcestershire sauce, vegetarian/vegan-friendly brands are available, such as Henderson's, Biona and Chippa.
d) I have changed the recipe slightly from the corresponding YouTube video. Mix powder has been increased from 1 to 1½ tsp, and Kashmiri chilli powder has been included as an option.

Shahee Chicken Tikka

The word 'Shahee' or 'Shahi' means 'Royal' in Hindi. When you see this word on the menu of an Indian restaurant or takeaway it will be for a curry which strives to be regal and elaborate, often with a mixture of different meats.

This is my take on a common theme, headlining with chicken tikka, keema, and a hard-boiled egg. It's a mild-medium curry by default, but of course you can spice it up with extra chilli powder if you wish.

With its generous meat and egg content this rich dish is enough to feed two people.

Ingredients

- 4 TBSP Oil (60ml)
- 1-2 Bay Leaves (Tej Patta Asian Bay preferred)
- 5-10cm Cassia Bark
- 2-3 Green Cardamom pods, split open
- 1 Star Anise (optional)
- 50-60g Onion, very finely chopped
- 25-30g Green Pepper, finely chopped
- 1½ tsp Ginger/Garlic Paste
- 1 tsp Kasuri Methi
- 1½ tsp Mix Powder
- ½ tsp Tandoori Masala
- ¼-½ tsp Salt
- ¼-1 tsp Chilli Powder (optional)
- 330ml+ Base Gravy, heated up
- 5 TBSP Tomato Paste
- 1 TBSP fresh Coriander Stalks, finely chopped
- 150g Chicken Tikka
- 100g pre-cooked Keema
- 1 Egg, small or medium, hard-boiled and peeled
- 3-4 splashes of Worcestershire Sauce (optional)
- 2-3 tsp Onion Paste (optional)
- ¼ tsp Orange Food Colouring (optional)
- 2 Tomato Segments
- ¼ tsp Garam Masala
- Fresh Coriander leaves for garnishing

Method

1. Firstly hard boil the egg for 8-10 minutes in salted water. Place in cold water to cool down, then peel it and set it aside for later.
2. Add the oil to a frying pan and heat up to medium high.
3. Add the bay leaves, cassia bark, green cardamom and the optional star anise, and fry for 30-40 seconds to infuse flavour into the oil, stirring frequently.
4. Now add the onion and green pepper. Fry for about 1–2 minutes until softened and the onions turn translucent. Stir from time to time to avoid burning.
5. Add the ginger/garlic paste and continue to cook for 20-30 seconds or until the sizzling starts turning into a subtle crackling sound. Stir frequently.
6. Next, add the kasuri methi, mix powder, salt, tandoori masala, and the optional chilli powder.
7. Fry for 20-30 seconds, stirring very frequently. If the mixture dries out and sticks to the pan, add a little base gravy (e.g. 30ml) to avoid burning the spices and to give them enough time to cook properly.
8. Add the tomato paste, coriander stalks, chicken tikka, and the keema. Turn up the heat to high, and mix well.
9. Add 75ml of base gravy, stir into the sauce, and leave on high heat with no further stirring until the sauce has reduced a little, tiny craters form around the edges, and there is some visible separation of oil.
10. Next, add a second 75ml of base gravy, stirring and scraping the bottom and sides of the pan once when first added, allowing the sauce to reduce again.
11. Then add 150ml of base gravy and the hard-boiled egg. An optional few splashes of Worcestershire sauce will add extra flavour, as will the onion paste.
12. For a slightly more vibrant look to this royal curry, add the orange food colouring.
13. Stir and scrape the pan, then leave to cook on high heat for 4-5 minutes. Stir and scrape once or twice to mix the

caramelised sauce back in, but do this only to prevent the sauce from sticking too much and burning. It's important to let the sauce adhere to the bottom and sides of the pan, which produces a fantastic flavour.

14. Put in the tomato segments a minute or two before the anticipated end of cooking.

15. If you want more sauce in the shahee, add extra base gravy near the end of cooking.
16. Shortly before the end of cooking, stir in the garam masala. Taste, and season as required. Spoon off the surface oil to reduce calorific intake.
17. Garnish with finely-chopped coriander.

Notes

a) If you want to use the optional onion paste the recipe can be found in Volume 1.
b) A full recipe for pre-cooked keema is also in Volume 1 of the book. For a shortcut compromise, fry the minced lamb, mutton or beef in a little oil with some mix powder, garam masala, and salt for 15-20 minutes, adding water to stop it drying out and burning.

Mango Chicken

The juicy sweet flavour of mango is wedded with tender chicken and accompanied by the ever-faithful coconut milk/powder, tangy lime juice, and a confetti of chaat masala. Oodles of fresh coriander help bring out the freshness of this mild-medium spiced curry.

Ingredients

- 3-4 TBSP (45-60ml) Oil
- 1½ tsp Ginger/Garlic Paste
- 1 tsp Kasuri Methi
- 1¼ tsp Mix Powder
- ¼ tsp Garam Masala
- ½-1 tsp Kashmiri Chilli Powder or ¼-½ tsp 'Regular' Chilli Powder (optional)
- ¼ tsp Salt
- 330ml+ Base Gravy, heated up
- 2-3 TBSP fresh Coriander Stalks, very finely chopped
- Pre-cooked Chicken or Chicken Tikka
- 2-3 tsp fresh Green Chilli, sliced horizontally (optional)
- 4 TBSP Coconut Powder (not desiccated) or 100ml Coconut Milk
- 4 TBSP Mango Pulp (tinned) or 1-2 TBSP Mango Chutney
- 120-150g fresh or tinned Mango, in cubes or slices
- 2 tsp Lime Juice. (Lemon will do)
- 2 TBSP fresh Coriander Leaves, finely chopped
- ¼ tsp Chaat Masala

Mango Chicken Tikka

Method

1. Add the oil to a frying pan and heat to medium high.
2. Add ginger/garlic paste and continue to cook for 30 seconds or until the sizzling subsides, stirring frequently to avoid burning.
3. Next, add the kasuri methi, mix powder, garam masala, salt, and the optional chilli powder.
4. Fry for 20-30 seconds, stirring very frequently. Add a little base gravy (e.g. 30ml) if the mixture dries out and sticks to the pan. This avoids burning the spices and gives them enough time to cook properly.
5. Add the coriander stalks, the pre-cooked chicken or chicken tikka, and the optional fresh chilli. Turn up the heat to high and coat the chicken well.
6. Add 75ml of base gravy, stir into the sauce, and leave on high heat with no further stirring until the sauce is reduced a little, and craters form again around the edges.
7. Next, add the coconut powder (if using) and a second 75ml of base gravy, stirring and scraping the bottom and sides of the pan once when first added, allowing the sauce to reduce again. The coconut powder soaks up a lot of liquid so add extra base gravy or water (e.g. 75ml) to allow it to dissolve.
8. Add 150ml of base gravy, mango pulp/chutney, fresh/tinned mango pieces, lime juice, and coconut milk (if using).
9. Stir and scrape the pan and leave to cook on high heat for 4-5 minutes. Stir and scrape once or twice to mix the caramelised sauce back in, but do this only to prevent the sauce from sticking too much and burning. It's important to let the sauce adhere to the bottom and sides of the pan, a technique which produces a great flavour.
10. Add a little extra base gravy if needed to achieve a final thinnish consistency. (This step may only be necessary if using coconut powder instead of coconut milk.)
11. Shortly before the end of cooking add the fresh coriander and the chaat masala.
12. Adjust to your taste with extra mango pulp/chutney, chaat masala, and/or jaggery/brown sugar.

Notes

a) Chaat masala is a powdered blend of spices that is used in Indian food (most often street food, snacks or fruit) before eating to further season it, and has a fabulous tangy flavour which comes mainly from the amchoor (dried unripe mango) powder, salt, and often 'black' salt (kala namak), the latter giving a sulphurous taste.

Pasanda

A fairly sweet, mild, rich and creamy curry, featuring coconut, almond, and ginger. Lamb is superb as the main ingredient in a pasanda curry, which mirrors the way that this North Indian dish is traditionally served. In this BIR version the extra optional touches of onion paste and red wine lift it beyond being a simpler sweet curry such as korma.

Ingredients

- 3 TBSP (45ml) Oil. Butter Ghee makes a decadent substitute
- 5-10cm Cassia Bark
- 2-3 Green Cardamom Pods, split open or just use the seeds from within
- 50-60g Onion, very finely chopped (approx. half a medium onion)
- 8-10 fresh Ginger Juliennes from a piece approx. 2-3cm long, peeled and finely sliced into long, very thin matchsticks
- ¾ tsp Mix Powder
- ¼ tsp Turmeric
- ¼ tsp Salt
- ¼ tsp Black Pepper, freshly ground
- 275-300ml+ Base Gravy, heated up
- 3 TBSP Coconut Powder/Flour (not desiccated)
- 2 TBSP Almond Powder
- 1½-2 TBSP White Sugar
- Pre-cooked Lamb, Chicken, Prawns, Vegetables, etc. Lamb is the traditional meat to use
- 2-3 tsp Onion Paste. (Optional. See Notes section)
- 30-40ml Red/White Wine. (Optional. Red wine is more 'authentic' in a Pasanda curry, but white wine may be used if preferred)
- ¼ tsp Garam Masala
- 100-125ml Single Cream, plus a little extra for garnishing
- A small Slice of Tomato
- 1-2 tsp Butter Ghee (optional)
- Pinch of Saffron (optional)

Method

1. Add the oil or ghee to the frying pan on medium high heat.
2. When hot, add the cassia bark and green cardamom. Fry for 30-45 seconds whilst stirring to infuse the oil.
3. Add the onion and fry for 1-2 minutes until soft and translucent.
4. Next add the ginger strips, mix powder, turmeric, salt, black pepper, coconut powder/flour, almond powder, white sugar, and 75ml of base gravy.
5. Fry for about a minute to cook the spices and to soften the coconut powder/flour. Within that time, add a little more base gravy or water (e.g. 50ml) when the mixture turns very thick to give the coconut more time to dissolve, and for the spices to cook through properly.
6. Now add the pre-cooked meat/vegetables/prawns, etc., 200ml of base gravy, and the optional onion paste. Turn the heat up to high and mix well.
7. Leave to cook on high heat for 3-4 minutes until the coconut and almond powders have dissolved, and oil can be seen floating on the surface. The sauce will thicken up quickly and will start to stick to the pan. Let it stick for a time to caramelise, but stir and scrape once or twice to prevent burning.
8. Add a bit of extra base gravy during that time if you wish. That will give the

Lamb Pasanda

coconut and almond powders time to meld properly into the sauce.

9. Then turn the heat down to low and add 100-125ml single cream and the 30-40ml red/white wine (optional). Return the heat to high once mixed in and leave to cook for a further minute.

10. Now taste the curry and add more sugar, cream or wine, as desired.

11. Add 1-2 tsp of butter ghee just before serving for extra flavour and richness (optional). If you are being health conscious then spoon any surplus oil from the top of the curry instead.

12. Serve, sprinkling on a small pinch of garam masala and drizzling a little extra cream on top. Finally, top with a piece of tomato.

13. For ultimate and voluntary decadence top with a pinch of saffron.

Notes

a) The recipe for the optional onion paste is detailed in Volume 1.

b) My associated recipe video for this pasanda differs slightly. This book's recipe includes different timings and a better explanation of using base gravy.

Restaurant Style Curries   81

Mr Naga

A very hot curry with Mr Naga chilli pickle taking centre stage as the star of the show. Mr Naga is a hot pickle with a special flavour that deserves serious credit, and is often used by Indian takeaways and restaurants as a condiment to enhance curries. You can buy Mr Naga in Asian grocery shops and supermarkets, or from the internet at a premium.

Ingredients

- 3-4 TBSP Oil (45-60ml)
- 1 tsp Cumin Seeds
- 2 tsp Ginger/Garlic Paste
- 1 tsp Kasuri Methi
- 1 tsp Extra Hot Chilli Powder (or 2 tsp 'regular' chilli powder)
- 1½ tsp Mix Powder
- ¼-½ tsp Salt
- 4-6 TBSP Tomato Paste
- 330ml+ Base Gravy, heated up
- Pre-cooked Chicken/Lamb/Vegetables, etc.
- 1 TBSP Mr Naga Chilli Pickle (adjust to taste)
- 1 fresh Naga Chilli, finely chopped (optional)
- 2-3 tsp Honey or Jaggery/Brown Sugar (optional)
- Fresh Coriander, Cucumber Slice, and some very fine Naga Chilli Slices for garnish

Method

1. Add the ghee/oil to frying pan on medium high heat.
2. Then add the cumin seeds and fry for 30-45 seconds, or until the seeds start to crackle. Stir frequently.
3. Next add the ginger/garlic paste and stir diligently until starting to brown and the sizzling sound reduces.
4. Add the kasuri methi, extra hot chilli powder, mix powder, salt, and a splash of base gravy (e.g. 30ml) to help the spices cook without burning.
5. Fry for 20-30 seconds, stirring frequently with the flat of the spoon.
6. Add the tomato paste and turn up the heat to high. Cook for 20-30 seconds or until the oil separates and tiny craters appear around the edges. Stir occasionally.
7. Now add the pre-cooked chicken/lamb/vegetables, etc., and mix well into the sauce.
8. Add 75ml of base gravy, stir into the sauce, and leave on high heat until the sauce has reduced a little and tiny craters form again. This should take 30 seconds or so.
9. Repeat the previous step by adding another 75ml of base gravy. Stir and scrape the bottom and sides of the pan once when first added, then leave the sauce to cook as before.
10. Add 150ml of base gravy and stir/scrape once again.
11. Leave to cook on high heat for 4-5 minutes or until the desired consistency is reached and the oil has separated. Halfway through that 4-5 minute period add the Mr Naga chilli pickle and the fresh naga chilli (if you are using it).
12. Add a bit more base gravy during cooking if desired to thin the sauce out to your preferred consistency. Stir and scrape the caramelisation back into the sauce,

but do this only once or twice to prevent burning.

13. Dare to taste the curry a minute or so before the end of cooking. Pour in the optional but recommended 2-3 tsp honey if desired. The honey gives a nice rounded flavour that works well with the sharpness of Mr Naga. If you have no honey, use jaggery or brown sugar.

14. Garnish with a slice of cucumber, finely chopped coriander leaves, and very thin slices of a red naga chilli.

Notes

a) Mr Naga is a must for this curry, but you can substitute a Scotch bonnet for the fresh Naga chilli if you wish to.

Mr Naga Keema

LavaStorm

Here's a magnificently spicy dish that goes beyond description on the heat scale. If you managed to eat the phaal curry in Volume 1 then you'll certainly find this one a greater challenge!

The curry, which I've aptly named 'LavaStorm', is inundated with numerous hot chillies, chilli flakes, and chilli powder. It has a delicious composition of various accompanying ingredients for an experience of great flavour, not just extreme heat.

The working title of this recipe was 'the curry that's so hot there's no word to describe it'. Good luck if you try this one. You'll need it!

Ingredients

- 5 TBSP (75ml) Oil or Ghee
- 10cm Cassia Bark
- 1 tsp Cumin Seeds
- 2 Green Cardamom Pods, split open
- 60g Finely Chopped Onion
- 30-40g Red Pepper, sliced (about quarter of one)
- 2 tsp Ginger/Garlic Paste
- 1 tsp Kasuri Methi
- 2 tsp Extra Hot Chilli Powder or 3-4 tsp 'regular' Chilli Powder
- 2 tsp Kashmiri Chilli Powder
- 1¼ tsp Mix Powder
- ¼-½ tsp Salt
- 6 TBSP Tomato Paste
- 3 TBSP Molten Lava Chilli Paste (see below)
- 1 TBSP Chilli Flakes
- 1-2 tsp Chilli/Naga Pickle (optional)
- 330ml+ Base Gravy, heated up
- Pre-cooked Chicken/Lamb/Beef/Vegetables, etc.
- 2-3 tsp Onion Paste (optional)
- 2 tsp fresh Lime or Lemon Juice
- 8-10 Green Chillies, finely sliced width-wise
- 2 tsp Honey & 1 tsp Sugar
- 1 TBSP Natural Yoghurt
- Fresh Coriander, finely chopped
- A Tomato Slice for garnishing

Molten Lava Chilli Paste

A blend of fresh garlic and various hot RED chillies. Feel free to experiment. For this recipe I blend the following ingredients with a little water. (Remove the membrane/seeds from the chillies for less heat.) This will make more than the 3 TBSP required for the curry recipe.

3 Garlic Cloves, 1 tsp Tandoori Masala

2 'Naga' Chillies, 4 Thai Red Chillies

2 Scotch Bonnet or Habanero Chillies

1-2 'regular' supermarket Red Chillies (medium heat)

Restaurant Style Curries

Method

1. Add the ghee and/or oil to a frying pan on medium high heat.
2. Add the cassia bark, cumin seeds, and cardamom pods. Fry for 30-45 seconds to infuse the oil, stirring frequently.
3. Add the finely chopped onion and sliced red pepper. Cook for 1-2 minutes or until the onions brown on the edges. Stir often.
4. Now add the ginger/garlic paste and fry for 15-25 seconds, or until the sizzling subsides.
5. Add the kasuri methi, chilli powders, mix powder, and salt. Pour over 30ml of base gravy to help mix the spices and prevent burning.
6. Fry for 30-40 seconds, stirring constantly and ensuring flat distribution of the spices in the pan. If the spices show signs of starting to stick to the pan and burning, add a little water or base gravy to loosen things up. It's very important to cook the spice powders out properly.
7. Add the tomato paste, molten lava chilli paste, chilli flakes, and the optional chilli/naga pickle. Turn up the heat to high and cook for 45 seconds while stirring diligently, until the oil separates and tiny craters appear.
8. Add the pre-cooked chicken/lamb/vegetables, etc., and mix well into the sauce.
9. Add 75ml of base gravy, stir into the sauce, and leave on high heat (avoiding stirring/scraping unless showing signs of imminent burning) until the sauce is reduced a little, and the craters form once again.
10. Add a second 75ml of base gravy, stir and scrape the bottom and sides of the pan once when first added, then allow the sauce to reduce again.
11. Now add the final 150ml of base gravy, fresh lime or lemon juice, honey, sugar, finely sliced green chillies, and the optional onion paste. Stir and scrape once when first added.
12. Leave to cook on high heat for 4-5 minutes, or until the desired consistency is reached. Add a little more base gravy if desired to thin the sauce out as to your preference. Avoid stirring/scraping unless the curry shows signs of starting to burn.
13. Taste the curry and cook for longer if evident that the chilli powders have not cooked out enough. Add more sugar, salt or lemon/lime juice as to your preference.
14. Just before the end of cooking turn the heat to low and stir in the natural yoghurt. This will help with appearance.
15. There should be a lot of excess oil on the surface. Spoon it off from the top of the curry if you want to be health conscious.
16. Serve, sprinkling the finely chopped coriander leaves on top, and garnishing with a slice or two of tomato.

Notes

a) When handling fresh chillies, use extreme caution. Wash your hands immediately afterwards and avoid touching your face or other sensitive parts.
b) The recipe for the optional onion paste is contained in Volume 1.
c) Caution is advised when cooking this curry. Ensure extractor fans in the kitchen are turned on full, and windows open. Wearing a mask is advised!
d) Misty Ricardo's Curry Kitchen is not accountable for any physical or psychological effects that may or may not occur during and after consuming a LavaStorm curry.

LavaStorm Chicken

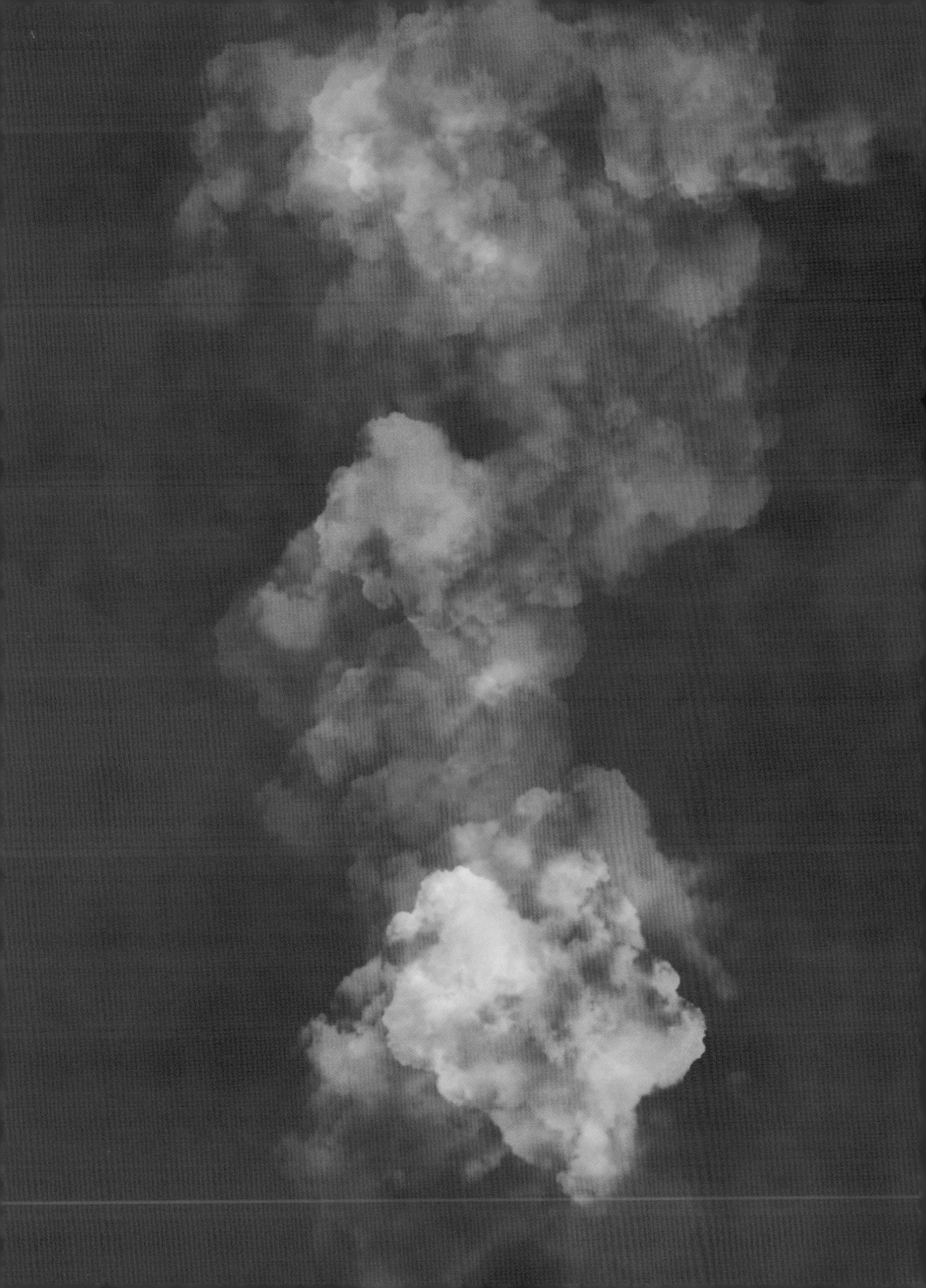

South Indian Tamarind

The flavours of tamarind, coconut milk, pickle and spices give this mild aromatic curry its special tang. An optional touch of jaggery or brown sugar balances the sour flavour.

I serve this curry in quite a lot of sauce, making it quite thin compared to other British Indian Restaurant style curries. It works well with chicken, but you can also use other meat, seafood or vegetables.

Ingredients

- 3 TBSP (45ml) Oil. Use Butter Ghee or Vegetable Ghee instead or in part for a richer, more rounded flavour
- 10cm Cassia Bark
- ½ tsp Cumin Seeds
- Seeds from 1 Black Cardamom (optional). Discard the outer pod
- 1½ tsp Ginger/Garlic Paste
- 1 tsp Kasuri Methi
- 1¼ tsp Mix Powder
- ¼-½ tsp Chilli Powder (optional)
- ¼-½ tsp Salt
- 380ml+ Base Gravy, heated up
- 3-4 TBSP Tomato Paste
- Pre-cooked Chicken, Tikka, Lamb, Prawns, Vegetables, etc.
- 1-2 tsp Jaggery or Brown Sugar (optional). This will balance the tartness of the tamarind and pickle. Note: bottled tamarind sauce is most likely to already contain sugar, so adjust to taste
- Tamarind, in one of the following forms:
  - 1¾ TBSP Tamarind Sauce (bottled commercial brand - East End, Maggi, etc.)
  - ¾-1 tsp Tamarind Concentrate
  - 2½ TBSP Tamarind Pulp (soaked, mashed, and strained from a block)
- 2 tsp Indian Pickle of your choice, chopped smooth to break down any bits
- 150ml Coconut Milk

Method

1. Add the oil/ghee to a frying pan and heat to medium high.
2. Now add the cassia bark, cumin seeds, and the optional black cardamom seeds (removed from the pod).
3. Cook for 30-40 seconds to infuse flavour into the oil, stirring frequently.
4. Next add the ginger/garlic paste and continue to cook for 20-30 seconds or until the sizzling sound lessens. Stir diligently.
5. Then add the kasuri methi, mix powder, salt, and the optional chilli powder.
6. Fry for 20-30 seconds, stirring very frequently. Add a splash of base gravy (e.g. 30ml) when the mixture dries out and starts to stick to the pan. This avoids burning the spices and gives them enough time to cook properly.
7. Now add the tomato paste and your choice of pre-cooked meat/vegetables, etc. Turn up the heat to high and mix well.
8. Add 75ml of base gravy, stir into the sauce, and leave on high heat with no further stirring until the sauce is reduced a little and craters form again around the edges.
9. Next add a second 75ml of base gravy, stirring and scraping the bottom and sides of the pan once when first added, and allow the sauce to reduce again.

South Indian Tamarind Chicken

10. Add 200ml of base gravy, the tamarind, pickle, coconut milk, and the optional jaggery or brown sugar.
11. Stir and scrape the pan and leave to cook on high heat for 4-5 minutes. Stir and scrape once or twice to mix the caramelised sauce back in, but do this only to prevent the sauce from sticking too much and burning. It's important to let the sauce adhere to the bottom and sides of the pan, which produces a great flavour.
12. Add extra base gravy if needed to achieve a final thin and smooth consistency.
13. Adjust to your taste with extra tamarind, sugar and/or pickle.

Restaurant Style Curries

Special Vegetarian Curries

Egg Bhuna

Let's face it, the notion of an egg curry needs a good sales pitch, so I heartily recommend that you try this one. You will never think of eggs in the same way again!

I've based my recipe on one given to me by Anwar Hussain, a Bangladeshi chef and restaurateur who (at the time of writing) owns the Cheddar Cottage restaurant in North Somerset. His version is fantastic, but I've tweaked it to my own preference mostly by adding a little tomato purée, cumin and garam masala, and have scaled the recipe down to a single portion size.

This dish uses neither base gravy nor mix powder, so it falls firmly within the 'home style' camp of Indian cooking. Give it a go – I'm optimistic that you will like it.

The recipe produces a decent-sized portion for one person or two to three as a side dish. You can double the ingredients if you wish, but tone down the spices and salt a little and cook for a bit longer.

Ingredients

- 3 small or medium Eggs. Free range taste better
- 1 TBSP Oil and ½ tsp Turmeric for colouring the Eggs
- 200g Onion (approx. 4 small or 2½ medium)
- 3 Garlic Cloves, finely diced
- 3-4 TBSP Oil for cooking the bhuna
- 2 Bay Leaves. Asian variety Tej Patta preferred
- ¾-1 TBSP Tomato Purée (double concentrated)
- ¼ tsp Chilli Powder
- 1 tsp Coriander Powder
- ½ tsp Cumin Powder
- ½ tsp Turmeric
- ¼ tsp Garam Masala
- ½ tsp Salt
- 2 fresh Green Chillies, sliced lengthwise
- Fresh Coriander, finely chopped
- 1 tsp Mango Chutney (optional)

Method

1. To start off simmer the eggs in salted boiling water for 8-10 minutes. Place the hard-boiled eggs in cold water to speed up the cooling process.
2. Carefully peel the eggs once they are cool enough to handle.
3. Then heat 1 TBSP of oil and ½ tsp of turmeric in a frying pan on low-medium. Put the eggs in and fry gently for a minute or two, turning them frequently until they turn an attractive orange colour all over. Scoop the eggs from the pan and set aside.
4. Now peel and roughly chop the onion and blend it to a smooth paste.
5. Add 3-4 TBSP oil to a non-stick frying pan on medium heat. Add the garlic and fry until golden brown, stirring often to prevent it burning.
6. Now add the bay leaves, blended onion, tomato purée, salt, and the powdered spices. Mix everything together.
7. Fry for a minute or two, and when the mixture starts bubbling like molten lava add 100ml of hot water. Turn the heat down to low and cook for 10 minutes or until all the water from the onion has

evaporated – the puffs of steam will become infrequent and the sauce will be very thick. Stir occasionally.
8. Then stir in another 100ml of hot water and leave to cook for 2-3 minutes.
9. Finally mix in the eggs, chopped coriander, green chilli, and, if you prefer a little sweetness, the mango chutney. Cook for another 2-3 minutes, stirring occasionally. The sauce is supposed to be very thick, but you can add extra water if you wish.
10. Serve garnished with fresh coriander.

Notes

a) For a posh effect on the hard-boiled eggs, vertically slice 1mm into each peeled egg 5 times before frying them. Anwar gives a clever tip – it's easier to do this with a piece of eggshell than a knife.
b) Use free range eggs for a superior taste.
c) Freshly prepared cumin and coriander powder have a superior flavour. Toast the whole seeds in a dry pan on low-medium heat for a minute then grind when cooled.

Spinach & Mushroom Balti

I have found that experimenting with leftovers can often be an inspiration for new recipes. This spinach & mushroom balti is a curry that I was pleased to chance upon.

The deliciously distinctive flavours of iron-rich spinach and the savoury umami of mushrooms are brought together and accentuated with a balanced mixture of ingredients to create a crowd-pleasing dish that works equally well as a main (for one) or a side (for two or more).

For authenticity cook and serve this curry in a korai or similar. I prefer to use an original Birmingham Balti Bowl to cook this curry, as the thin pressed steel transfers a lot of heat while cooking and imparts a distinctive and delicious taste to the balti.

Ingredients

- 4 TBSP (60ml) Oil
- 250g Raw Spinach
- ½ tsp Salt (in two stages)
- Pinch of Black Pepper
- 150g Mushrooms of your choice, halved or quartered
- 1 tsp Kasuri Methi
- 5cm Cassia Bark
- 1 tsp Panch Phoran
- 3 Green Cardamom Pods, split open
- ¼-½ tsp Ajwain Seeds (aka Carom)
- 50g Onion, finely chopped
- 2 Garlic Cloves, finely sliced
- 2cm fresh Ginger piece, finely sliced
- 30g Red Pepper, roughly chopped
- 1 tsp Mix Powder
- ¼ tsp Garam Masala
- ¼ tsp Chilli Powder (optional)
- 225ml+ Base Gravy, heated up
- 5–6 TBSP Tomato Paste
- 3-4 TBSP fresh Coriander Stalks, finely chopped
- ¼-½ tsp Tamarind Concentrate or 1 tsp Lemon Juice
- Tomato Segments & fresh Coriander to garnish
- 1-2 tsp Butter Ghee (optional)

Method

1. Firstly, prepare the spinach, which will then be put to one side and added back into the dish towards the end of cooking. Heat 1 TBSP of oil in a medium or large sized pan, and add the raw spinach, ¼ tsp of the salt, and a pinch of ground black pepper.
2. Cook for a couple of minutes or until the spinach goes soft and wilts to a fraction of its original volume. Stir occasionally.
3. Remove the spinach, drain, and squeeze all the excess liquid from it. Chop it up finely.
4. Heat the remaining 3 TBSP of oil in a balti bowl, korai, wok, or frying pan on medium high setting.
5. Add the mushrooms and kasuri methi, and stir fry for 2 minutes to brown them. It is normal for the mushroom pieces to shrink in size as they release water. Scoop the mushrooms out and set aside.
6. Then to the same pan add the cassia bark, panch phoran, split green cardamom pods, and the ajwain seeds. Fry the whole spices for 30 seconds to infuse the oil with flavour.

Spinach & Mushroom Balti

7. Add the onion, garlic, ginger, and red pepper. Fry for a further minute, stirring sensibly.
8. Now, add the mix powder, garam masala, ¼ tsp salt, and the chilli powder (if using).
9. Fry for 20-30 seconds, stirring very frequently. Add a splash of base gravy (e.g. 30ml) if the mixture dries out. This avoids burning the spices and gives them enough time to cook properly.
10. Next add the tomato paste, the tamarind/lemon juice, the coriander stalks, and turn the heat up to high.
11. Add the wilted and squeezed spinach and mix together well.
12. Leave to cook for a minute. The spinach will still contain water, which will need to be evaporated.
13. Now add in 75ml base gravy, stir once, and leave to cook until the sauce is reduced a little and small craters form again around the edges of the pan.
14. Add a second 75ml base gravy. Stir then leave to cook for a further minute or two until the craters form again.
15. Add a third 75ml of base gravy and the pre-cooked mushrooms. Stir once again and leave to cook down for 4-5 minutes. Avoid stirring during this time to let the sauce caramelise on the sides and bottom, and intervene only if you become worried about it burning.
16. Taste and add extra salt if desired.
17. Top with 1–2 tsp of butter ghee just before serving and mix gently. The ghee will add a rich flavour and give the balti an attractive appearance.
18. Finally, serve in the pan you cooked it in, garnished with fresh coriander and tomato segments. Serve with naan bread for best results.

Notes

a) For more information about the Birmingham Balti Bowl, visit https://thebirminghambaltibowlco.com/

Punjabi Vegetable 'Staff' Curry

Here's an awesome traditional-style vegetable curry made with cauliflower and potatoes. I've based this recipe on the one demonstrated to me by Alex Wilkie in his Glaswegian kitchen. He was keen to share this recipe with me, having originally been given it by a Punjabi chef with whom he worked at an Indian takeaway.

I was at first dubious about this dish, but experienced a revelation once I tasted it. The first word that came to mind (after 'awesome') was 'meaty'. The firm texture of the potato and cauliflower combined with the punchy sauce make this a fascinating and moreish curry.

This recipe will feed three to four people and lasts forever when used as a side dish. Works best alongside other dishes.

Ingredients

- 2-3 TBSP (30-45ml) Oil for browning the Potato and Cauliflower
- 400-450g Baby Potatoes, cut in half with the skin left on
- 400g Cauliflower, cut into medium large florets (approx. 1 medium Cauliflower)
- 6-8 TBSP (135ml) Oil for making the curry
- 425g Onion, peeled and chopped (approx. 500g unpeeled weight)
- 1 TBSP Cumin Seeds
- 1 TBSP Fennel Seeds
- 2-3 Bay Leaves. Asian variety (Tej Patta) preferable, but you can use European ones instead
- 4 Green Cardamom, split open
- 6 Black Peppercorns, crushed (use the back of a large knife or a pestle & mortar)
- 1½ tsp Coriander Seeds, crushed
- 10cm Cassia Bark
- 2-3 Green Chillies, finely chopped (optional)
- 2½ TBSP Ginger/Garlic Paste
- 180-200g fresh Vine Tomatoes, cut into small chunks (approx. 2-3 large tomatoes)
- 2-3 TBSP fresh Coriander Stalks, finely chopped
- 2½ tsp Salt
- 1½ TBSP Kasuri Methi
- 3 tsp Turmeric
- 1½ tsp Kashmiri Chilli Powder or Deggi Mirch (see Notes)
- 2 tsp Garam Masala
- 1 TBSP Brown Sugar or Jaggery
- 2½-3 TBSP Tomato Purée (double concentrated)
- 1 TBSP Lemon Juice
- 2-3 TBSP fresh Coriander Leaves, finely chopped

Method

1. First we're going to brown the potato and cauliflower pieces to enhance the flavour.
2. Add 2-3 TBSP of oil to a large frying pan, wok, or korai on high heat. Add the potato and cauliflower pieces when the oil is hot. Toss them around to coat in the oil then fry for 10 minutes, mixing them around every couple of minutes. If you don't have a cooking vessel big enough then you can fry them in batches.
3. When the potato and cauliflower pieces are nicely brown and caramelised, remove them and set aside for later.
4. Now add the 6-8 TBSP of oil to a saucepan or pot of no less than 4L capacity on medium heat. Aluminium or steel pans are best for this recipe because they facilitate caramelisation better than those with a non-stick coating.
5. When the oil has heated up add the chopped onion, cumin seeds, fennel seeds, bay leaves, green cardamom, the crushed black peppercorns and coriander seeds, and the cassia bark.
6. Leave to fry until most of the onion has turned brown. The process will take some time, perhaps up to 30 minutes. Adding a little of the salt at this stage will draw out the water in the onions and speed up the cooking process. If you do add salt now, remember to reduce the amount added later on. Periodically add a splash of water to deglaze the bottom of the pan when you see dark brown caramelised bits sticking to the bottom, and stir back in to give the onions more time to cook down without catching and burning.
7. Now add in the finely chopped green chillies if you want a little heat and extra flavour.

8. Next add the ginger/garlic paste. Fry for a further 45 seconds to cook out the raw flavour, stirring frequently.
9. Now turn up the heat and stir in the fresh tomato chunks, chopped coriander stalks, salt, kasuri methi, turmeric, chilli powder, garam masala and the sugar/jaggery. Fry the spices for 30-40 seconds whilst stirring diligently.
10. Add the tomato purée, lemon juice, and the potato pieces. Mix and coat everything together. Note that the cauliflower hasn't been added yet because it takes less time to cook than potato.
11. Then pour in enough hot water to barely cover, stir once, and bring to a low simmer. Partially cover the pan and leave for 15 minutes.
12. Stir in the cauliflower pieces and leave to cook for a further 10-15 minutes. The curry should end up with a medium thickness, so if it appears too watery at this point remove the lid from the pan to help the steam escape. Conversely, add a little more water if it appears too thick.
13. The trick is to end up with the right consistency and to have the vegetables firm but tender. Test the potato and cauliflower after the 10-15 minutes and cook for a little longer if too firm. Don't overcook the cauliflower or it will turn mushy.
14. There will likely be a considerable amount of oil floating on top of the curry, which can be taken off the surface with a spoon as desired.
15. Finally, remove the whole spices and stir in the chopped fresh coriander leaves. It's now ready to serve.

Notes

a) If you like the idea of a slowly cooked bone-in staff chicken curry, you will find a splendid recipe in INDIAN RESTAURANT CURRY AT HOME Volume 1.
b) The recipe has been tweaked slightly from that demonstrated in the accompanying YouTube video. I have increased the amount of cauliflower and added extra whole garam masala spices at the beginning of cooking in place of the powder shown in the video.

Chana Masala

Chickpeas are incredibly popular throughout South Asia and beyond. As with all pulses they are relatively cheap and packed with protein, so they form an important part of the diet, especially for vegetarians and vegans.

Chana masala (referred to as 'chole' in Punjabi cuisine) is a famous Indian chickpea dish, and is an example of how basic, cheap ingredients can be turned into a hearty, nourishing meal with amazing tastes and textures. Amchoor (dried unripe mango) powder is traditionally used as a souring agent, although lemon juice can be used as a less preferable substitute.

The balance of sweetness in my recipe comes from the very thick and caramelised base gravy.

This recipe serves one person as a main course or two to three as a side dish.

Ingredients

- 3 TBSP (45ml) Oil
- ½ tsp Cumin Seeds
- ½ tsp Mustard Seeds
- 100g Onion, cut thinly into semi-circular or quarter-circle slices
- 1½ tsp Ginger/Garlic Paste
- 1 tsp Kasuri Methi
- 1½ tsp Mix Powder
- ½-1 tsp Kashmiri Chilli Powder
- ¼ tsp Garam Masala
- ½ tsp Salt
- 280ml+ Base Gravy, heated up
- 4 TBSP Tomato Paste
- 200-250g cooked Chickpeas. A 400g tin contains the required amount when drained. You can use dry Chickpeas but they will need soaking overnight and cooking first (see Notes below)
- 2 TBSP Coriander Stalks, very finely chopped
- 1½ tsp Lemon Juice
- 1-3 fresh Green Chilli, thinly chopped widthwise (optional)
- 2-3 tsp Onion Paste (optional)
- 2 fresh Tomato quarters
- ¾ tsp Amchoor (sour Mango) Powder (optional)
- 2 tsp fresh Ginger, thinly sliced into matchstick shapes (optional)
- Fresh Coriander Leaf, finely chopped (for garnishing)

Special Vegetarian Curries

Method

1. Add the oil to a frying pan on medium high heat.
2. Add the cumin seeds and mustard seeds. Stir diligently for 30-45 seconds to infuse the oil with flavour, or until the mustard seeds start popping.
3. Next add the onion. Fry for a minute or two until softened but not browned, stirring often.
4. Now put in the ginger/garlic paste, stirring until the sizzling subsides.
5. Add the Kasuri methi, mix powder, Kashmiri chilli powder, garam masala, salt, and a small amount of base gravy (e.g. 30ml) to help the spices fry without burning.
6. Fry for 20-30 seconds, stirring constantly.
7. Add the tomato paste. Turn up the heat to high while stirring constantly for 30-40 seconds, or until the oil separates and tiny craters appear.
8. Add the chickpeas and the coriander stalks. Mix well into the sauce.
9. Now add the first 75ml of base gravy, stir into the sauce, and leave on high heat (not stirring) until the sauce has reduced a little, and craters form again.
10. Add a second 75ml of base gravy, stirring and scraping the bottom and sides of the pan once when first added, and allowing the sauce to reduce again.
11. Add the lemon juice and the optional green chilli and onion paste.
12. Now add 100ml of base gravy. Stir and scrape once when first added.
13. Leave to cook on high heat for 4-5 minutes, or until the sauce becomes very thick and the chickpeas have softened. Add a little extra base gravy if desired to thin the sauce out, as to your preference. Avoid stirring/scraping unless the curry shows signs of imminently starting to burn.
14. Put in the fresh tomato and the optional amchoor powder a couple of minutes before the end of cooking.
15. Taste and add more salt or lemon juice/dressing if desired.
16. Serve garnished with fresh coriander and the optional ginger juliennes.

Notes

a) If you are starting off with dry chickpeas you must first soak them overnight in plenty of water, and then simmer them for 1-1½ hours, or until tender.
b) The recipe for the optional onion paste can be found in Volume 1.

Saag Paneer

A classic vegetarian dish with spinach and chunks of Indian cottage cheese (paneer). Fresh tasting and vibrant green in colour, it's ideally eaten as a side dish to other contrasting curries. 'Saag' in Hindi means 'leafy vegetable', so can refer to spinach, coriander, fenugreek/methi, etc. The dish is also commonly known as 'palak' paneer, with 'palak' specifically meaning spinach.

You can make your own paneer instead of buying it if you wish. The shop-bought version tends to be a safer bet, as it's consistently firm and holds its shape well.

Ingredients

- 60ml Oil
- 180g Paneer
- 150-180g fresh Spinach, including stalks. Frozen blocks of Spinach (defrosted) can be used instead
- 3-4 TBSP fresh Coriander, including the stalks
- 1-2 Green Chillies (optional)
- ½ tsp Cumin Seeds
- 1 Bay Leaf (optional). Tej Patta (Asian Bay) preferred, but a few 'normal' smaller bay leaves may be used instead
- 75-90g Onion, very finely chopped
- 1½ tsp Ginger/Garlic Paste
- 1 tsp Kasuri Methi
- ¾ tsp Mix Powder
- ¼ tsp Garam Masala
- ½ tsp Salt
- 4 TBSP Tomato Paste
- 275-300ml+ Base Gravy, heated up
- 1 tsp Sugar
- 1 tsp Lemon Juice or 1 tsp Mint Sauce
- 75-100ml Single Cream

Method

1. Cut the paneer into cubes approximately 2-3cm in width.
2. In a non-stick frying pan on medium high heat, add 1 TBSP of the oil (15ml) and fry the paneer until browned on several sides. Turn the cubes during cooking but be careful not to break them. Place them aside on kitchen towel to remove excess oil.
3. Wilt the spinach in a pan with a little water, then blend it with the fresh coriander and optional green chillies to form a smooth paste. Use a little oil or water to help blending if required.
4. Add the remainder (3 TBSP, 45ml) of the oil to your usual curry frying pan on medium high heat.
5. Throw in the cumin seeds and Asian bay leaf (if using), then fry for 30-45 seconds or until the cumin seeds start crackling.
6. Now add the onion and continue frying for 1-2 minutes until soft and translucent, but not browned. Stir occasionally.
7. Add the ginger/garlic paste. Fry for 30-45 seconds or until the sizzling subsides and the paste is just starting to brown very slightly.
8. Then add the kasuri methi, mix powder, garam masala, and salt.
9. Fry for 20-30 seconds, stirring diligently. If the powders start to stick to the pan, add a splash of base gravy (e.g. 30ml) to prevent burning and to give the spices long enough to cook correctly.

10. Turn up the heat to high and add the tomato paste. Stir in and leave to fry 30 seconds or so to bring out the tomato flavour. You should notice a bit of oil floating on the surface.
11. Next add the first 75ml of base gravy and stir into the sauce. Leave for 30–40 seconds, or until small craters have formed and caramelisation is visible on the sides of the frying pan.
12. Now add a second 75ml base gravy and repeat the previous stage.
13. Then add the spinach/coriander/chilli paste, paneer cubes, lemon juice or mint sauce, sugar, along with a third 75ml of base gravy. Scrape and stir the contents of the frying pan well.
14. Leave to cook on high heat for 3-4 minutes, adding extra base gravy or water during cooking to maintain a medium consistency. Resist fiddling with it: let the sauce stick and caramelise further, but don't let it burn.
15. Next, turn the heat down and add 75-100ml single cream. Return heat to high once mixed in. Cook for a further 1-2 minutes, until the sauce reduces to a medium consistency.
16. Taste, and if desired add a little sugar, lemon/mint, and/or extra salt, to taste.
17. Serve, sprinkling on fresh coriander and optionally drizzle with a little extra cream. Place a single raw spinach leaf in the centre for extra green bling!

Notes

a) The saag paneer should have a vibrant green colour naturally given by the spinach and contrasted by the whiteness of the cheese.

Kadai Paneer

Kadai paneer is a mouth-watering dish that's served in a very thick sauce, made with mild, creamy Indian cottage cheese (paneer), peppers, onions, and a balance of well-suited spices and herbs.

Keep an eye out for paneer when you next find yourself at the cheese counter of a supermarket. Paneer is used abundantly in vegetarian Indian cooking. It's made simply from the separated curds of whole milk, which are heavily compressed then cut into cubes once firmed up fully.

Whilst not having much more than a creamy flavour, paneer takes on the flavours of its accompanying ingredients. That, along with its firm and 'pleasing in the mouth' texture, makes this a surprisingly delicious and satisfying main course.

No base gravy or mix powder is required in my recipe. Serves one to two.

Ingredients

- 175-200g Paneer, cut into 2 cm cubes
- 100-120g Green Pepper, cut into 2-3cm triangles (approx. half a large Pepper)
- 120-150g Onion, cut into 2-3cm segments (approx. 1 medium Onion)
- 2 tsp Kasuri Methi (Dried Fenugreek Leaves)
- 3 TBSP (45ml) Oil
- ½ tsp Cumin Seeds
- 2-3 tsp Ginger/Garlic Paste
- 1 TBSP Tomato Purée (double concentrated) with a little water to dilute, or 125-150g fresh Tomatoes, finely chopped
- 2 TBSP fresh Coriander Stalks, finely chopped
- ½ tsp Cumin & ½ tsp Coriander Powder. Toast and grind seeds for the best flavour
- ¼ tsp Turmeric
- Pinch of Garam Masala (about one eighth tsp)
- ½ tsp Tandoori Masala
- ¾ tsp Curry Powder (e.g. Mild Madras)
- ½-1 tsp Kashmiri Chilli Powder, for colour and warmth (optional)
- ½ tsp Salt
- 1–2 tsp Lemon Juice
- 1–2 tsp fresh Green Chilli, finely chopped (optional)
- 2 TBSP fresh Coriander Leaves, finely chopped
- ¼ tsp Chaat Masala

Method

1. Coat the paneer chunks well with 1-2 tsp of the oil, 1 tsp of the kasuri methi, and a sprinkle of salt. Ensure you use firm paneer. Home-made paneer can often be too crumbly, so use shop-bought unless you have mastered the art of making it.
2. Similarly, in a separate receptacle, mix the green pepper and onion with the same amount of oil, the other 1 tsp of kasuri methi, and the salt.
3. Heat a non-stick frying pan or tawa on high. The non-stick properties will prevent the paneer sticking.
4. Add 1 TBSP of oil, the paneer, and fry for 1-2 minutes, stirring gently to avoid it breaking up. Allow the paneer to turn dark brown on a few of the sides of the cubes. Remove and set aside until later.
5. Next add the remaining 1 TBSP of oil to a korai, wok, or balti pan on highest heat. Throw in the pepper and onion mixture and fry for 2-3 minutes, stirring frequently. Let the surface of the pepper and onion pieces char to develop a smoky flavour.

6. Now add the cumin seeds and ginger/garlic paste. Fry for 30-45 seconds, stirring frequently.
7. Then spoon in the fresh tomato (or diluted tomato purée) and the coriander stalks. Continue cooking for a further 30 seconds.
8. Next add the cumin and coriander powder, turmeric, garam masala, tandoori masala, curry powder, salt, and the optional Kashmiri chilli powder. Also add 3 TBSP of water to loosen things up a little.
9. Stir-fry for another minute to allow the spices to cook through, then add the fried paneer cubes, lemon juice, and the optional chopped green chilli.
10. Now leave to cook for 7-9 minutes, stirring occasionally. Add a little water (or base gravy if you have some) along the way to avoid the contents sticking and burning. Keep the sauce thick and allow it to caramelise on the edges of the pan. The final consistency should be very thick - ideal for scooping up with chapati or naan.
11. Just before the end of cooking add the chopped coriander leaves and ¼ tsp chaat masala.
12. Taste and if desired add more salt or chaat masala.
13. Serve enthusiastically, directly from the korai/wok (if safe and suitable), a very hot serving korai dish, or cast-iron sizzler platter. You could just dump it into a bowl instead.

Notes

a) Chaat masala is a powdered blend of spices that is used in Indian food (most often street food, snacks or fruit) before eating to further season it. Chaat masala has a fabulous zingy flavour, which comes mainly from the amchoor (dried unripe mango) powder, salt, and often 'black' salt (kala namak), the latter giving a sulphurous taste.

Rice

Lemon Rice

You may have noticed lemon rice in the 'rice & sundries' section of Indian restaurant and takeaway menus. It's yet another hidden gem which is sadly disregarded. My version uses both lemon juice and the essential lemon rind, along with some unconventional spices which I think complement the zesty flavour of this fried rice accompaniment.

This recipe will make enough for one or two people when served alongside a main dish. If you wish to make extra it's best to repeat the recipe each time instead of scaling up. It's quick to cook and the results are well worth it!

Ingredients

- 200g Cooked Basmati Rice (left to dry/cool so not moist)
- 2 TBSP (30ml) Oil or Ghee
- ½ tsp Black Cumin Seeds (see Notes)
- ½ tsp Black Mustard Seeds
- ¼ tsp Hing aka Asafoetida (optional, see Notes)
- 60g Onion, roughly chopped (about half of a medium one)
- 2 Garlic Cloves, finely sliced
- 1-2 tsp finely chopped fresh Green Chilli (optional)
- ¼-½ tsp Salt
- 1 tsp Mix Powder
- ½ tsp Turmeric
- ½ tsp Tandoori Masala
- ½ tsp Kalonji Seeds (also known as Nigella)
- 1-2 tsp Lemon Rind (finely grated or chopped)
- 2 TBSP fresh Coriander Leaves, finely chopped
- 1 TBSP fresh Lemon Juice
- 1-2 tsp Butter Ghee to finish (optional)

Method

1. Cook the basmati rice according to the instructions on the packet or your preferred method. Make sure any excess water is drained, then run a fork through it gently a few times and leave to dry off a bit and cool. Don't leave rice at room temperature for more than an hour or so. If in doubt place the rice container in ice cold water or refrigerate after cooking.
2. Heat the oil or ghee in a wok or frying pan on high heat.
3. Add the black cumin seeds, the black mustard seeds, and the optional hing.
4. When the mustard seeds start popping add the chopped onion and 2 garlic cloves.
5. Stir fry for 30-45 seconds or until the onion browns at the edges. The sweetness of the partly caramelised onion will complement the sharpness of the lemon.
6. Now add the salt, mix powder, turmeric, tandoori masala, kalonji seeds, and the optional green chilli.
7. Continue frying for 20-30 seconds stirring diligently to prevent the spices from sticking and burning.
8. Then add the lemon rind, the cooked basmati rice and the chopped coriander leaf.
9. Mix together well and continue stir frying for a minimum of 90 seconds until the rice is piping hot.
10. Add the fresh lemon juice shortly before the end of cooking, and if you wish, top with some butter ghee for extra richness.
11. Serve, sprinkling a little bit more fresh coriander on top.

Notes

a) Never leave cooked rice at room temperature for more than an hour or two. If not using immediately, always cool and refrigerate, or keep hot.
b) Black cumin seeds (Hindi: kala zeera) are slightly smaller and thinner than the common brown variety, and impart a smoky, earthy flavour when cooked. They can be bought from most South Asian food shops, but if you can't get hold of some then 1 tsp of 'regular' cumin may be used instead.
c) The use of hing is optional (it may be hard to come by in some places). It adds a taste like onion and garlic and works well in this dish.
d) Check the amount of salt in your cooked basmati rice. If it was cooked using salt (especially with the absorption method), then adjust the amount of salt when frying.
e) This recipe differs slightly from the one shown in the accompanying YouTube Video in that the coriander stalks have been removed and the lemon rind increased from 1 tsp to 1-2 tsp.

Cumin & Onion Pilau

Sometimes simplicity is the key to the most excellent flavour. This delicious pilau rice has few ingredients yet maximises their potential and is quick and easy to cook.

This recipe will feed three or four people as part of a meal. Scale it up or down according to how much you wish to make.

Ingredients

- 1½ TBSP Oil or Vegetable Ghee
- 2 TBSP Cumin Seeds
- 200g Onion, finely chopped (approx. 240g unpeeled weight or 2 medium Onions)
- 2 Garlic Cloves, thinly sliced
- ½-¾ tsp Salt
- 300ml / 320g Basmati Rice, uncooked
- ½ tsp Cumin Powder
- Hot Water

Method

1. Gently rinse the basmati in cold water and drain the liquid. Repeat five or more times or until the drained water is almost clear.
2. Add the oil or ghee to a non-stick frying pan on medium heat.
3. When the oil is hot, add the cumin seeds and fry for 20-30 seconds.
4. Next add the sliced garlic, chopped onion, and the salt. Fry for 2-3 minutes until the onion has softened and browned slightly. Stir regularly.
5. Now add the basmati rice and cumin powder. Continue frying for another 2 minutes or until all the grains of rice have turned white.
6. Pour in 300ml of hot water and mix gently. Turn the heat down to low and cover the frying pan. Leave to cook for 6-7 minutes without lifting the lid.
7. After that simply turn off the heat and let the pilau rest (still covered) for 5 minutes or until you wish to serve it.

Notes

a) Any surplus pilau can be stored in the fridge for a few days or frozen for a few months.

b) Don't leave cooked rice at room temperature for long. If you are storing it then cool it down quickly first.

c) A 'mainstream' pilau rice recipe is in Volume 1 of INDIAN RESTAURANT CURRY AT HOME, or you can find the video recipe on the Misty Ricardo's Curry Kitchen YouTube channel.

Street Food & Other Oddities

Chilli & Tomato Chutney

Condiments such as this chilli and tomato chutney are easy to make and superior in taste to their shop-bought counterparts. You can make this relish as mild or hot as you like simply by adjusting the amount and type of fresh chillies. For all you chilli growers out there this is an excellent way of using them up. (Thanks to my friend Graham Warburton for the generous selection of pods.)

This recipe will make about 400-450ml of chutney.

Ingredients

- 4 TBSP Oil
- 2 tsp Black Mustard Seeds
- 180g Onion, finely sliced (approx. 2 small-medium ones)
- 1 tsp Salt
- 5 Garlic Cloves, finely chopped
- 1½ tsp Cumin Powder (freshly ground)
- 2 tsp Coriander Powder (freshly ground)
- ½ tsp Turmeric
- 1 tsp Kashmiri Chilli Powder
- 1 tsp Paprika
- ¼ tsp Garam Masala
- 20-100g Chillies, chopped (as mild or hot as you like)
- 400g fresh Tomatoes, roughly chopped
- 1½ TBSP Sugar
- 1 TBSP Vinegar

Method

1. Add the oil to a saucepan on medium heat.
2. Add the mustard seeds when the oil is hot and wait until they start to crackle and pop.
3. Then put in the chopped onions and the salt. Fry for 6-8 minutes or until the onion has softened and is almost starting to brown. Stir frequently.
4. Next add the garlic and fry for a further minute whilst continuing to stir often.
5. Add the cumin powder, coriander powder, turmeric, Kashmiri chilli powder, paprika, and the garam masala. Mix and keep stirring diligently for 1-1½ minutes while the spice powders fry. Add a splash of water if they start to cling to the saucepan to give them more time to cook properly without burning.
6. Now put in the chopped tomatoes and chillies. Stir everything together while scraping the bottom of the pan - the acidity in the tomato will deglaze the surface.
7. Continue to cook for 2 minutes, stirring diligently to stop the mixture catching and burning.
8. Then stir in 100ml of hot water, cover the pan, and turn the heat down to low-medium.
9. Leave to cook for 15 minutes but stir once or twice during that time.
10. Remove from the heat, add the sugar and vinegar, then blend until fully smooth. I find using a stick blender is easier than a food processor or jug blender as there's less washing up to do.
11. Put the saucepan with the blended chutney back on a low heat and simmer for 30 minutes, stirring occasionally. The chutney should end up thick but pourable. Add a little water to thin it down if desired.

12. Allow to cool a little then pour into sterilised glass containers and seal.
13. Can be eaten immediately but will improve over time as the flavours get familiar with each other.
14. Refrigerate when at room temperature. I estimate the chutney will stay pukka for about two weeks if kept cold, but, like me, you will probably have consumed it all by then anyway.

Green Chutney

This coriander-based condiment is used abundantly across India, and surprisingly it has not gained mainstream popularity in British Indian Restaurants. I love eating this chutney with poppadoms, as its sharp freshness contrasts wonderfully with sweeter accompaniments such as mango chutney and raita.

There are many variations of green chutney, but the most common constituents are fresh coriander leaves, salt, and lemon juice. Some other common ingredients are green chilli, fresh mint, garlic, ginger, cumin powder, chaat masala, and sugar.

When I first ate this healthy and fresh concoction in Mumbai, it was with a succulent piece of tandoori chicken leg. From that moment I was a fan. It's an essential accompaniment to street food in India, most notably the Bombay sandwich and masala toast (see page 124 for my recipe).

My version focuses on the basics but includes options for more sophisticated palates. This recipe will make about 5 TBSP (75ml) of green chutney, and of course the ingredients can be scaled accordingly to make a larger amount if you prefer.

Ingredients

- 1 Metric Cup (250ml) fresh Coriander Leaves
- ½ Metric Cup (125ml) fresh Mint Leaves
- 1-1½ tsp Lemon Juice
- ¼ tsp Salt
- 1 tsp Sugar
- ½ Garlic Clove
- ½-1 Green Chilli (optional)
- ½ cm cube of Ginger, peeled (optional)
- ¼ tsp Toasted Cumin Powder (optional)
- ¼ tsp Chaat Masala (optional)

Method

1. Roughly chop all the solid ingredients, combine with the other ingredients plus a splash of water, then blend to a fine paste.

Notes

a) The toasted cumin powder is prepared firstly by heating cumin seeds in a dry frying pan on low-medium heat until they have darkened and a heady aroma is released. Once cooled, grind the toasted seeds to a powder with a coffee/spice grinder or pestle & mortar.

b) Green chutney with mint is usually referred to as 'Mint Chutney'.

c) The green chutney will last for a few days in the refrigerator or it can be frozen if preferred.

d) Various commercial brands and types of bottled green chutney sauces are available to buy in most Asian food shops and supermarkets.

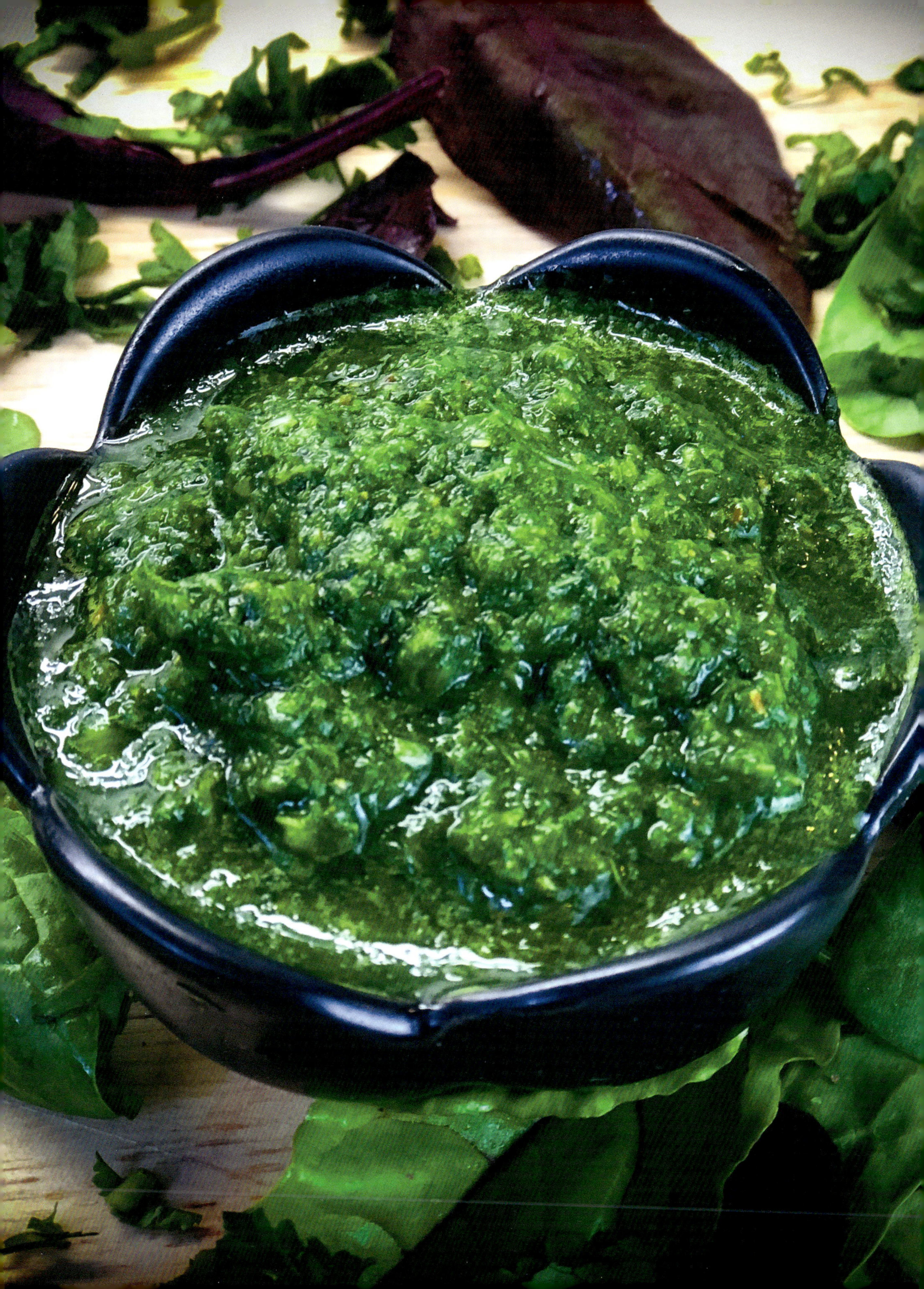

Chicken 65

Chicken 65 is one of the classic dishes of South Indian cuisine. It's a spicy deep-fried chicken dish with a tangy, thick sauce, and is most often eaten as a starter or street food snack.

The dish originates from the South Eastern Indian city of Chennai (formerly Madras) in the Tamil Nadu state. There are many strange rumours and claims as to how the dish acquired its name. For example, some say that 65 chickens are needed to make the dish, or that it was listed on a roadside vendor's menu as number 65.

The Times of India newspaper says that it was created by A.M. Buhari, founder of the Buhari Hotel in Chennai, in 1965. The hotel restaurant followed the naming convention by subsequently introducing Chicken 78, 82 and 90, each corresponding to the years they were introduced.

Take your pick as to which version you believe, but rest assured you only need 400g of chicken to make this recipe, which will yield four starter/snack portions, or two main course portions.

Ingredients

For the Battered Chicken

- 400g Chicken Breast, Thigh or Leg (cleaned, boneless, skinless)
- 1½ tsp Ginger/Garlic Paste
- 1 tsp Lemon Juice
- ½ tsp Salt
- ½ tsp Garam Masala
- 1 tsp Kashmiri Chilli Powder
- 1 tsp Fennel Seeds
- 1 tsp Paprika
- 1½ tsp Tandoori Masala Powder OR 1 tsp Tandoori Masala Paste (commercial brand)
- 3-4 TBSP Cornflour
- 1 TBSP All-Purpose Flour
- Oil for deep-frying

For the Sauce

- 45ml Oil (Vegetable/Sunflower, etc.)
- ¾ tsp Cumin Seeds
- ½ tsp Mustard Seeds
- 1 TBSP fresh or 2 TBSP Dried Curry Leaves (optional)
- 80g Onion, finely diced
- 40g Green Pepper, finely diced
- 1½ tsp Ginger/Garlic Paste
- 1 tsp Kasuri Methi
- 1½ tsp Tandoori Masala Powder or 1 tsp Tandoori Masala Paste (commercial brand)
- ¼-½ tsp Turmeric
- 1 tsp Coriander Powder (freshly toasted and ground is best)
- 1 tsp Curry Powder (for example mild Madras curry powder)
- 1 tsp Paprika
- 1 tsp Kashmiri Chilli Powder
- ¼ tsp Salt
- 2½ TBSP Tomato Ketchup
- 1 tsp Dark Soy Sauce
- 1 tsp Lemon Juice or Dressing
- Pinch of Red Food Colouring (optional)
- 1-2 tsp fresh Red Chilli, finely chopped (optional)
- 3 TBSP (45ml) Yoghurt (full fat)
- 2-3 tsp Honey

Method

For the Battered Chicken

1. Chop the chicken into small pieces, about 2-3 cm in diameter. Try to cut each piece about the same size.
2. Add the chicken pieces and all the other batter ingredients except for the flours into a bowl and mix well with clean hands. Set aside for a minimum of 2 hours.
3. Then add both types of flour and a little water to the bowl to form a very thick paste. Stir well to ensure chicken is evenly coated. You may need to add a little more cornflour or water to get the right thickness.
4. Heat a medium-large pan no more than half-filled with oil to 170-180°C. A temperature gun or a cooking thermometer comes in handy here. Alternatively, you can use a deep fat fryer if you have one. For obvious reasons care and attention need to be paid when deep frying.
5. The chicken pieces need to be cooked in small batches. For this 400g recipe two or three batches will be enough. If too much is placed in the oil the temperature will drop too far and the batter will be soggy and won't stick to the chicken properly.
6. Place a batch of the battered chicken gently into the hot oil. Allow to settle for a few seconds, then gently stir with a heat-resistant spoon.
7. Leave to deep fry for 4-5 minutes or until dark and crispy but not burnt. Stir and

Street Food & Other Oddities

turn the chicken pieces a few times while they are cooking.

8. Scoop out the chicken pieces and drain on kitchen towel. Cover and keep them warm to help them stay crispy. Repeat for the remaining batches, making sure the oil temperature is 170-180°C, as stated earlier.

For the Sauce

1. Now it's time to make a sauce to coat those posh Indian chicken nuggets. Add 3 TBSP (45ml) of oil to a frying pan on medium high heat.
2. Next add the cumin seeds, mustard seeds, and the curry leaves (if using). Fry for 30-45 seconds or until the mustard seeds start popping.
3. Now add the finely diced onion and green pepper and fry for 2-3 minutes until soft, translucent, and just starting to brown around the edges.
4. Add the ginger/garlic paste. Fry for 30 seconds or until the sizzling subsides and the paste is just starting to change colour.
5. Add the kasuri methi, tandoori masala powder or paste, turmeric, coriander powder, curry powder, paprika, Kashmiri chilli powder, and salt.
6. Fry for 20-30 seconds, initially adding 30ml of water to help the spices cook properly without burning. Stir frequently.
7. Then add about 75ml more water, stir, and leave to cook for a further minute, stirring/scraping only if the sauce shows signs of sticking and burning.
8. Now turn the heat up to high and add the tomato ketchup, dark soy sauce, lemon juice, the optional red food colouring, optional red chilli, and a further 75ml water. Stir together and a leave to cook for a further couple of minutes.
9. Turn the heat to low temporarily before adding the yoghurt and honey. Once mixed in turn the heat back up to high and leave to cook for a further minute or two until the sauce is thick. Taste and add more salt, lemon juice and/or honey if desired.
10. Add the battered chicken pieces and mix.
11. Serve with slices of onion and wedges of lemon. Best eaten immediately while the chicken is still crispy.

Notes

a) You can use either breast or thigh meat for this dish. I recommend using chicken thigh for a better flavour and a chewy texture.
b) Always keep raw chicken away from other ingredients, and thoroughly clean everything that it's been in contact with before cooking with it.
c) Curry leaves work well in this dish. I urge you to buy some fresh curry leaves as the flavour is much better, but dried are satisfactory.
d) The red food colouring is optional but gives the Chicken 65 a great look. The Kashmiri chilli powder and paprika give off a nice red colour too, so you might decide not to use the food colouring as well.
e) To impress your friends and family, serve on a super-hot cast iron sizzle platter with lightly oiled semi-circular onion rings and a squeeze of lemon juice for a smoky effect.
f) This recipe varies a touch from the corresponding YouTube video. I have increased the spicing a bit and increased the amount of cornflour used.

Bunny Chow

Bunny chow originates from Durban, South Africa, where the immigrant Indian population invented a cheap street food meal during hard economic times. Originally vegetables were mostly used instead of meat, but the modern bunny chow is typically a spicy lamb curry with lots of gravy served inside half a loaf of bread, accompanied by a pickled carrot salad. For the more authentic experience eat with hands only, using the scooped-out bread as a dip.

I hesitate to use the word 'dish' to describe bunny chow. It's less elegant than that and takes pride in being messy. So, what's with the name? There is absolutely no connection with rabbits. A popular theory is that Indians from the Bania caste created the 'dish' to serve as an easy to carry takeaway, which was passed through café windows to those excluded from entering the premises.

This recipe will make enough curry to feed three to four people. Feel free to experiment with the size and the type of bread you serve it in – half a large loaf will most likely be too big a serving size for one person unless shared (that would get messy!).

Ingredients

- 125ml Oil, Ghee, or a combination
- 2 Asian Bay Leaves (Tej Patta). European Bay Leaves can be used instead
- 10cm Cassia Bark
- 1 Star Anise
- 1 tsp Cumin Seeds
- 1 tsp Black Mustard Seeds
- 1 tsp Fennel Seeds
- A small handful of fresh Curry Leaves, crushed (optional, see Notes section)
- 300g Onion, chopped (approx. 3 medium-sized ones)
- 20g Garlic Cloves, minced or very finely chopped (about 6 cloves)
- 10g Ginger, also minced or finely chopped
- 1 tsp Turmeric
- 1 tsp Coriander Powder (freshly toasted and ground from seeds)
- 3 tsp Curry Powder (e.g. mild Madras)
- 1 tsp Cayenne Pepper or Extra Hot Chilli Powder
- 2 tsp Kashmiri Chilli Powder
- 1½ tsp Salt
- ¼ tsp Black Pepper (freshly ground)
- 400g Lamb diced into 2-3cm cubes, with any spare bones. Mutton, goat, or beef can be used instead. Come to think of it, so can rabbit
- Half a 400g tin of Plum Tomatoes or 200g of fresh ones
- 3 TBSP Tomato Purée (double concentrated)
- 4-6 TBSP fresh Coriander Stalks, finely chopped
- 2-3 Green Chillies, finely chopped (optional, to taste)
- 100g Potato, peeled and diced into small cubes (approx. half a medium one)
- 200-300g additional Vegetables (optional). For example, a handful of sliced carrot, aubergine, courgette, green beans, red pepper, cauliflower, chickpeas, etc.
- 200-250ml Water
- 1 Loaf of White Bread, unsliced and cuboid shaped, or crusty cob rolls if serving smaller individual portions.

For the Carrot Salad:

- 1 Medium Large Carrot, grated
- ½ small-medium Onion, very finely chopped
- ½ Tomato, chopped
- Coriander Leaf, handful, very finely chopped
- 1-2 TBSP Vinegar of decent quality
- 1 Green Chilli, very finely chopped (optional)

Method

1. Add the oil/ghee to a large pan (I suggest one of 4-5 litre minimum capacity) on medium heat.
2. Add the bay leaves, cassia bark and star anise, and stir into the oil for 30 seconds. Then add the spice seeds (cumin, mustard, and fennel) and stir frequently until the mustard seeds start popping.
3. Then add the chopped onion. Stir from time to time until the onions soften, turn translucent, and begin to brown (about 5-6 minutes). If the onions start to stick to the bottom of the pan add a little water and de-glaze the surface.
4. If you are using the curry leaves add them now. They should start crackling quite quickly.
5. Now throw in the minced garlic and ginger and cook for a further few minutes, stirring frequently.
6. Next add the turmeric, coriander powder, curry powder, cayenne/chilli powder,

Kashmiri chilli powder, salt, and black pepper. Mix well and cook for a couple of minutes, stirring diligently. If the spices start sticking to the pan, add a splash of water to deglaze and to allow the spices longer to cook through correctly for that time.

7. Slam the lamb in the pan and fry for a couple of minutes more, coating the lamb well and letting it brown a little. Also add any lamb bones you have spare to improve the flavour of the dish.
8. Slosh in the plum tomatoes, tomato ketchup, and the fresh coriander stalks. Mix well again.
9. Add the potato cubes, 200-250ml water, and the optional green chilli and/or other vegetables.
10. One further mix, then turn heat to low, cover the pan and leave to cook for 1-1½ hours, or until the lamb is tender. The sauce should not be thick, so add a little water to ensure a thinnish consistency. You want the sauce to soak into bread and ooze out if you make a hole in the side.
11. Taste and add extra salt and/or sugar to taste. A dollop of mango chutney works very well in place of sugar.
12. Remove the whole spices and bones (if using) and stir in a handful of chopped fresh coriander just before serving.
13. Now for the weird bit (if you are not familiar with bunny chow). Slice the bread loaf 4-5 inches from one end, so you get a square(ish) chunk with the crust at one end.
14. Place the loaf crust end down and scoop out enough of the inner bread to leave a generous hole, but keep the inside thick enough to soak up the curry without falling apart.
15. Spoon or ladle the curry into the hole until brimming. Serve with a carrot salad (see below) and some of the bread that was scooped out.
16. Eat, using the bread topping to dip in. Cutlery is not allowed – that would just be silly!
17. For the carrot salad, mix together the grated carrot, onion, tomato, coriander, vinegar, and optional green chilli. Be careful not to overdo the vinegar.

Notes

a) For a sensible and individual-sized portion, use a large crusty cob roll instead of a loaf.
b) Use fresh curry leaves for this in preference to dried. The fresh variety has so much more flavour. Curry leaves can be expensive and hard to get hold of, which is why I've listed them as optional.
c) No rabbits need be harmed during the production of this recipe.

Masala Toast

Masala toast, also known as a Bombay masala toast, is a common street food snack in India. Thick, buttered, toasted bread slices are spread with green chutney and filled with potato, onion, coriander, and other good things. Healthy, cheap, and easy to make, it makes a substantial lunch or a late-night treat.

You can add any other vegetables you wish to the filling. For instance, green pepper, peas, and tomato slices.

This recipe makes enough filling for two large sandwiches (four slices of bread). Best served freshly cooked while still warm. You can halve the ingredients if you just want to make a single sandwich.

Ingredients

- 200g Potatoes (unpeeled weight)
- 4 Slices of Thick White Bread
- 2-3 TBSP Unsalted Butter, Ghee, or Oil
- ½ tsp Cumin Seeds
- ½ tsp Panch Phoran
- 60g Onion, finely chopped
- 25g Red Pepper, finely chopped
- 1½ tsp Ginger/Garlic Paste
- ¼ tsp Garam Masala
- ¼ tsp Turmeric
- ½ tsp Chaat Masala or Salt
- ¼ tsp Chilli Powder (optional)
- 80g Tomato, finely chopped (approx. 1 medium Tomato)
- 1 tsp Lemon Juice
- 1 fresh Green Chilli, finely chopped (optional)
- 2 TBSP fresh Coriander Leaf, finely chopped
- Unsalted Butter (for spreading)
- Green Chutney (see Notes section)

Method

1. Peel and chop the potatoes into 2cm cubes. Add them along with 1 tsp turmeric and ½ tsp salt to a pan with plenty of boiling water. Whole spices such as bay leaf, cassia and cloves can also be added to infuse extra flavour into the potato.
2. Simmer for 15 minutes then drain and mash the potato chunks to a smooth consistency. Set aside for later. The resultant weight of the mashed potato should be approximately 175g.
3. While the potatoes are simmering, heat a non-stick frying pan to medium and toast each slice of bread on one side until golden brown. Set aside.
4. Then wipe the frying pan clean and place back on the hob on medium heat. Add the unsalted butter, ghee, or oil.
5. When hot add the cumin seeds and panch phoran. Fry until the mustard seeds within the panch phoran start to crackle and pop, while stirring frequently.
6. Next add the chopped onion and red pepper. Fry for 2 minutes or until the onion starts to brown around the edges.
7. Add the ginger/garlic paste and cook for a further 30-40 seconds to cook the raw flavour out.
8. Now put in the garam masala, turmeric, chaat masala or salt, and the optional chilli powder.

9. Fry for 30-40 seconds or so, stirring diligently. Add a splash of water to quench the powders to prevent burning and to give the spices more time to cook properly.
10. Then add the chopped tomato, lemon juice, and the optional chopped green chilli. Fry for a minute until the mixture has thickened. Stir frequently.
11. Add the mashed potato and the chopped fresh coriander. Mix everything together well and mash any remaining potato lumps. Cook for a further minute on low heat.
12. Taste the mixture and add extra salt or chaat masala if desired.
13. It's now time to assemble the sandwiches. Spread the untoasted side of each bread slice generously with unsalted butter.
14. Turn each slice butter-side down, then spread each toasted side with green chutney (see Notes section).
15. Then spoon about half the cooked filling on top of one slice of each sandwich. Spread evenly and top with another slice of the bread, chutney-side down.
16. Now it's time to fry the sandwich. Wipe the frying pan clean again and put it back on medium heat.
17. Once the pan is hot carefully place a sandwich into the dry pan.
18. Leave to fry for 2 minutes or until the underside is a nice darkish golden brown. Turn the slice over and cook the other side for 2 minutes. Repeat the stage for the second sandwich.
19. Best served immediately while still hot. Tomato ketchup and green chutney are great accompaniments to dip the masala toast sandwiches into.

Notes

a) You can find the recipe for green chutney on page 116.
b) Chaat masala is a blend of pungent spices which is very commonly used with Indian street food. It's salt-based and has sour keynote flavours from amchoor powder (dried unripe mango) and black salt, among others. It's available to buy in South Asian food shops and sometimes from larger mainstream supermarkets. Don't be without it!
c) Feel free to experiment with other vegetables – masala toast is very versatile. A mild grated cheese such as paneer or mozzarella can be added during the assembly stage for super-deliciousness.

Bassar Fried Chicken

All meat eaters love fried chicken, right? Try this recipe, which in my opinion gives KFC a serious run for its money. There are no secret ingredients here - it features a Pakistani masala called bassar, and its pungent, spicy flavour nicely augments the fried chicken to make it finger-licking good!

The recipe should make enough for three to four people as a snack or starter, but I'd play safe and make extra – it doesn't last long! Scale the ingredients up accordingly.

Ingredients

The Marinade

- 500g Chicken Thighs, boneless and skinless (approximately 4 thighs)
- 300ml Buttermilk or Yoghurt
- 100ml Milk
- 1½ TBSP Ginger/Garlic Paste
- 1 tsp Bassar Curry Powder (see Notes)
- 1 tsp Salt
- 2 tsp Fennel Seeds (optional)

The Coating

- 75g Plain Flour
- 75g Cornmeal/Polenta
- 1¼ TBSP Bassar Curry Powder
- 1 tsp Salt
- 1 TBSP Paprika
- 1 tsp Turmeric
- 2 tsp Sugar

Method

1. Mix the buttermilk/yoghurt, milk, ginger/garlic paste, bassar curry powder, salt, and the optional fennel seeds in a bowl.
2. Trim the chicken thighs of excess fat then place into the bowl and thoroughly coat with the marinade.
3. Cover and refrigerate for at least 4 hours. Overnight is better.
4. Before frying the chicken remove the bowl from the fridge and let it come near to room temperature for 30-45 minutes.
5. Mix the coating ingredients together in another bowl.
6. Lift a chicken thigh from the marinade bowl and dip it into the spiced flour mixture, making sure the chicken is fully coated. Then dip it back into the first bowl to cover with the marinade, and finally dip again in the flour to coat a second time.
7. Repeat the previous stage for the remainder of the chicken thighs.
8. Pour a 1½cm depth of oil into a large frying pan on high heat. Wait for the oil temperature to reach about 160°C. A cooking thermometer is very useful here.
9. Carefully place the chicken pieces into the oil. The temperature of the oil will drop considerably at this point, but it will gradually increase back up over time.
10. Leave to fry for 6 minutes before turning the pieces over and cooking for another 6 minutes. Keep an eye on the oil temperature while cooking, and turn the heat down a bit if it rises up to about 160°C again. That will help prevent the chicken from burning on the outside before it's fully cooked inside.
11. Test that the inner thigh meat has been correctly cooked (minimum 75°C) by using a temperature probe. Alternatively cut a piece in half and check that there are no pink or translucent parts. Fry the chicken for a minute or two longer if required then test again.
12. Drain on kitchen towel then devour at will while hot and crunchy. It goes well with a tangy tomato-based chutney and/or a cooling mint raita.

Notes

a) Bassar curry powder has its origins in Pakistan and Kashmir, and is widely used by Asian communities around the world. It's potent stuff, containing a high proportion of chilli powder as well as generous amounts of other pungent spices. You can buy various brands of bassar from Asian food shops and supermarkets, usually in 100g or 400g bags.

b) Chicken thighs vary in size. For this recipe I've assumed each thigh weighs about 100g based on a 500g pack from a supermarket containing five pieces. Larger thighs will need a little longer to cook thoroughly, or they can be cut in half (before marinating).

c) You can use breast meat instead of thigh if you prefer. You can also use bone-in cuts of chicken, in which case reduce the starting oil temperature to about 160°C and fry for 20 minutes in total, or until fully cooked inside.

d) The temperatures and timings are the same if you prefer to deep-fry the chicken.

e) Take care when handling raw chicken. Keep it well away from all other foodstuffs to avoid cross-contamination, and clean all surfaces and utensils that may have come into contact directly or indirectly during preparation.

Homestyle Lamb Curry

A traditional-style 'bone in' lamb curry that's cooked slowly in one pot for remarkable depth and breadth of flavour. This recipe demonstrates a typical style of cooking curry in South Asian households, and also in British Indian Restaurant kitchens, where it's often referred to as a 'staff curry'. As the name implies, this isn't for customers but for restaurant staff, and is eaten at or near the end of a shift. I'm glad to see that some restaurants have started to list their staff curry on the customer menu, and rightly so. It's delicious.

There are few real words that can be used to adequately describe the magical flavour of a meat-based curry cooked with the bones. I think it's best to just listen to the impulsive animal-like utterances of your family or friends when you cook this Misty Ricardo special dish for them. And please do – they will thank you for it!

Serves four. No base gravy or mix powder is used in this recipe.

Ingredients

- 180ml Oil
- 4 Asian Bay Leaves (Tej Patta). European Bay Leaves may be used instead but have a different flavour.
- 10cm Cassia Bark
- 6 Green Cardamom Pods, split open (or just use the seeds inside from within the pods)
- 4 Cloves
- 350g Onion, chopped (approx. 3 medium ones)
- 20g Garlic Cloves, minced or very finely chopped (about 6 cloves)
- 10g Ginger, also minced or very finely chopped
- 600-700g Lean Lamb Leg Meat, cut into 2-3cm pieces
- 300-400g Lamb Bones cut into large chunks (see Notes)
- 1 TBSP Kasuri Methi
- 1½ TBSP Cumin Seeds
- 1 TBSP Coriander Powder, freshly ground from seeds
- 1 tsp Turmeric
- 2 tsp Paprika
- 1½ tsp Garam Masala
- 1½ tsp Salt
- 1 tsp Chilli Powder (optional)
- 1 TBSP Fennel Seeds (optional)
- 16 TBSP Tomato Paste (see Notes)
- 4-6 TBSP fresh Coriander Stalks, finely chopped
- 200g Potato, peeled and diced into small cubes (approx. 1-2 medium sized ones)
- Any other Vegetables you fancy, e.g. Aubergine, Carrot, Squash, Pepper (optional)
- 4-6 fresh Green Chillies, chopped (optional)
- 300ml Water
- A handful of fresh Coriander Leaves, finely chopped
- 1-1½ TBSP Butter Ghee (optional)

Street Food & Other Oddities

Method

1. Add the oil to a large saucepan or pot (I suggest one of 5 litre minimum capacity) on low-medium heat.
2. When the oil has heated up throw in the Asian bay leaves, cassia bark, cardamom pods, and cloves. Stir into the oil for 45-60 seconds to start infusing flavour.
3. Add the chopped onion. Fry gently until the onions melt down and turn a golden brown. Stir frequently and be patient as it will take some time, perhaps up to 20-30 minutes. When the onions start to stick to the bottom of the pan, add a little water and de-glaze the surface. Repeat this process as often as needed until the onions are nicely browned.
4. Then add the garlic and ginger and fry for a further couple of minutes, stirring diligently.
5. Add the kasuri methi, cumin seeds, coriander powder, turmeric, paprika, garam masala, salt, and the optional chilli powder and fennel seeds. Mix together well and cook for a few minutes, once again stirring diligently to prevent anything sticking to the pan and burning.
6. Next add the pieces of lamb and the bones. Turn up the heat to medium high and mix it all together well. Cook for 5 minutes until the lamb has browned and has sealed, stirring frequently.
7. Now add the tomato paste, potato cubes, fresh coriander stalks, 300ml of water,

and the optional green chillies and/or other chosen vegetables.
8. Mix once again, bring back to a simmer, then cover and leave to cook on a low heat for 90 minutes, stirring from time to time to stop the sauce sticking to the pan and burning. No additional water should be necessary.
9. After the 90 minutes if the sauce is thin, cook uncovered on a slightly higher heat for 5-10 minutes until thickened.
10. Taste the sauce and add extra salt if desired, and add extra salt and/or sugar to taste.
11. Test the lamb for tenderness by gently stabbing a piece with a fork. If the lamb doesn't surrender and bleat 'eat me', re-cover the pan and continue cooking for another 15 minutes, after which you can retest it.
12. Scoop out the lamb bones and discard. You might also want to retrieve the whole spices (see Notes).
13. Finally, stir in a generous handful of chopped fresh coriander leaves. If you want a richer taste, melt in the butter ghee.
14. Serve with chapati, naan, or rice.

Notes

a) I strongly endorse the use of lamb bones in this dish - they augment the curry with an extra-special flavour. A 1kg leg of lamb has about the amount of lean meat needed for this recipe, so buy one from your butcher. Ask him or her to trim the fat, strip the meat from the bone, cube it, and chop the bones.

b) Beef, mutton, goat, or other red meats can be used instead of lamb for this curry. Make sure you still use bones for the added flavour. Other types of meats may take less or more time to cook. Adjust accordingly.

c) Tomato paste, as with every recipe in this book, is either blended plum tomatoes (tinned or fresh) or double-concentrated tomato purée diluted with three times its amount of water. For this recipe that would mean 4 TBSP tomato purée with 12 TBSP (180ml) of water, or ½-¾ of a 400g tin of blended plum tomatoes.

d) You will have noticed the abundance of whole garam masala spices used in this curry. For convenience you can leave them in when serving the curry, but to play safe scoop the whole spices out beforehand. The cassia bark and bay leaves are the easy pickings - good luck with the cardamom and cloves!

e) This lamb curry can be cooked in a pressure cooker from stage 8 onwards. Adjust the amount of water added from 300ml to 250ml in stage 7. Seal the cooker after mixing, bring it to high pressure, then leave for 20 minutes before releasing the pressure. Subsequently if the meat is still not tender or the sauce is runny you can simmer it further until ready.

Mango Lassi

A cold, refreshing yoghurt-based drink is welcome when the weather is hot, or if you need to tame the heat of a spicy curry. Lassi is popular all over the Indian subcontinent in both sweet and salty variations. I've tried salt lassi in India, which I'm confident is an 'acquired taste', so instead I have created a recipe for a sweet version featuring mango.

Ingredients

- 250ml Natural Yoghurt (cold)
- 400ml Milk (cold)
- 150-200ml Water (cold)
- 250ml Mango Pulp (see Notes)
- 2 tsp Lime or Lemon Juice
- 2 TBSP Sugar
- 3-5 Green Cardamom Pods
- Ice Cubes (a generous handful)
- A few strands of Saffron (optional)

Method

1. Crack open the green cardamom pods with the back of a knife, extract the seeds, and discard the outer husks. Crush the seeds using the blade of a knife or with a pestle and mortar. Pre-ground elachi (green cardamom) powder can be used instead, but the flavour will not be quite as good.
2. Add the yoghurt, milk, water, mango pulp, lime/lemon juice, sugar and the crushed green cardamom seeds into a jug or blender. Blend until smooth and frothy.
3. Add the ice cubes. Blend further if you want the ice to be crushed.
4. Pour into a glass, drizzle on some extra mango pulp, and optionally top with a few strands of saffron.

Notes

a) Mango pulp (mashed up blended and sweetened mango flesh) is usually sold in tins, which are readily available from Asian food shops and most of the larger mainstream supermarkets. There are many different varieties of the mango fruit, and you are likely to notice different types of pulp sold (for example Alphonso and Kesar). There is some debate about which one is best, although the Alphonso variety gets some good press.
b) You can use fresh mango as a superior substitute for the pulp, in which case you may want to add extra sugar to get the desired level of sweetness in your lassi.
c) The lassi will keep in the fridge for 2-3 days.

Cheesy Peas

"Now why didn't I think of that!" This is an expression I use once in a blue moon, but the utterance was especially pronounced when a friend (who we will call Rod) showed me his superb recipe for cheesy peas. Yes, matar paneer (peas with mild cottage cheese) is a popular and original favourite in the realm of traditional Indian cooking, but I'd never have imagined that a strong cheddar cheese would work in a BIR-style dish with the likes of base gravy and robust spices.

You may also initially baulk at the whole idea of it. However, I dare you to try cheesy peas or 'matar paneer á la cheddar' as Rod, a Scottish ex-pat living in France, might say.

Mange tout, Rodney, but if you have any leftovers they are spectacular on toast for breakfast. (Speaking of cheese on toast, do take a look at my next recipe - Chilli Cheese Toast on page 134.)

This recipe will feed two cheese fiends as a snack or starter. Great with naan, pitta, chapati, tortilla chips, or a soft white bread roll.

Ingredients

- 30ml Oil
- 1 tsp Butter Ghee or Unsalted Butter
- 60g Onion, finely chopped
- 2 tsp Ginger/Garlic Paste
- 1½-2 tsp Cumin Seeds
- ½ tsp Kasuri Methi
- 1¼ tsp Mix Powder
- 150ml Base Gravy
- 120g Peas, defrosted from frozen. Petit Pois have a sweetness that goes well in this recipe
- 80ml Single Cream
- 80-100g Grated Cheese. For flavour I recommend a strong cheddar, but you could use any cheese you like or indeed a combination
- 60g Tomato, finely cubed
- 1 TBSP fresh Coriander Leaves, finely chopped
- 2 fresh Green Chillies, finely chopped (optional)
- ½ tsp Chaat Masala

Method

1. Heat the oil and ghee/butter in a non-stick wok or frying pan on low-medium setting.
2. Add the finely chopped onion and fry for a minute until soft and translucent but not browned, stirring frequently.
3. Increase the heat to medium then throw in the cumin seeds and the ginger/garlic paste. Stir diligently while frying for 20-30 seconds or until the sizzling sound lessens and crackling sound increases.
4. Next put in the kasuri methi and the mix powder. No salt is added because the cheese we will be using is salty enough. Fry for 20-30 seconds, stirring frequently.
5. Then pour in 75ml of base gravy, stir once, and turn the heat up to medium high.
6. Leave to cook for a minute then add another 75ml of base gravy and the defrosted peas. Stir once again and cook for 3 minutes, stirring half way through.
7. Turn the heat to low then stir in the single cream.
8. Now it's time to add the grated cheese. Stir in gradually in handful-size amounts,

allowing each handful to distribute and melt into the sauce.

9. Add the tomato and the coriander. If you like a bit of a kick then also add the fresh green chilli.
10. Stir well, turn the heat up slightly to low-medium, and leave to cook for 2 minutes. Do not worry about the sauce being quite thin – it will thicken up when it has been served and cooled a little.
11. Finally stir in the chaat masala, taste for seasoning, and add a little salt if desired.
12. Serve and enjoy.

Chilli Cheese Toast

This quick and easy chilli cheese toast snack is fantastic any time, but is a proper treat after a boozy night out!

Ingredients

- 2 Slices of White or Brown Bread, thin or medium sliced
- 100-120g Grated Cheese. Mature Cheddar Cheese and Mozzarella are a good combination of flavour and texture
- 2 TBSP Red Pepper, finely cubed
- 2 Garlic Cloves, very finely chopped
- 2-3 fresh Green or Red Chillies, very finely chopped. Remove the membrane and seeds inside the chillies for less heat
- ¼ tsp Black Pepper, freshly ground
- ¼ tsp Chaat Masala
- ½ tsp Paprika
- A few splashes of Worcestershire Sauce

Method

1. Mix all the ingredients except for the bread and butter together in a bowl.
2. Toast one side of the bread slices under a hot grill or in a dry non-stick frying pan.
3. Spread the mixture generously onto the untoasted side of the bread slices. Make sure to cover the entire area of the bread including the sides and corners.
4. Place on a rack under a 180°C pre-heated grill and leave for 2-3 minutes or until the topping is deep golden brown and all the cheese has melted.
5. Eat. Simple!

Upscaling Curry

A Common Query

Of all the questions that crop up about British Indian Restaurant cooking, the most common one I'm asked is about upscaling - making more than one portion of any given curry at a time. Of course, people often want to cook the same dish for two or more people without the inconvenience of making the same single recipe-sized portion repeatedly. That's hardly surprising, and it's a subject area that merits a lot of explanation or at least a detailed 'perspective' from the author.

So, in this chapter I will be performing a 'brain dump' of my experiences, observations, and opinions. Scaling recipes up is more of an art than a science, but I will explain some key elements that need to be considered and provide some examples. That said, I feel it's important to stress my opinion that cooking BIR style in single recipe portions is preferable to scaling up, mainly because a higher temperature can be reached.

Volume 1 of INDIAN RESTAURANT CURRY AT HOME contains an abundance of information about heat control and the associated cooking methods for single recipe portion BIR curries.

A Note about Portion Sizes

Most of this book's curry recipes yield an amount about the same as you would expect from an Indian takeaway, and alongside accompaniments such as rice, is usually larger than the average person can eat in one meal. That is something to consider when scaling recipes up, because a double recipe portion may be just enough to feed three people. Likewise, a triple recipe portion may feed four or five, and so on.

Just to clarify, I use the words 'recipe portion' throughout this chapter to identify the amount of curry that a single recipe produces, and not the amount that someone eats as a serving. The multiples 'x2','x3','x4','x6' and so on denote the upscaled size of a single recipe portion.

The Heat Dilemma

Mostly it's about TEMPERATURE. The magical flavour that comes with good BIR curry is largely down to the high temperature level that ingredients in the cooking vessel can reach. Chemical processes such as caramelisation and the Maillard reaction happen at these high temperatures, and these reactions produce flavour compounds which improve the taste of a curry. A curry cooked without the temperature needed to release those flavour compounds may taste OK, but it will usually be inferior to one that is made with the higher heat.

The more ingredients added to a cooking vessel the greater the heat energy required to raise and/or maintain temperature. In a home kitchen the typical heat source (i.e. gas or electric hob) has limited output, and on 'full whack' is (just) enough to cook an excellent tasting SINGLE recipe portion BIR curry when using the right techniques. Make a double recipe portion using the same hob and what happens? The extra ingredients added to the pan cap the maximum temperature that can be reached and maintained, thus hindering the chemical reactions. Things are further hindered if a larger pan is required to hold the extra volume. The larger the pan the heavier it is, and the more energy it requires to attain – and maintain – high temperature.

That's the dilemma. The best heat output that can be reasonably expected from a standard domestic four-ring hob is about 3 kWh (kilowatts per hour), possibly 4 kWh for hobs with a special 'wok-ring' gas burner. If we had more powerful hobs in our kitchens then scaling recipes up would be less problematic, as we'd be able to match the heat source to an appropriate recipe size and scale up happily (subject to ingredient ratios).

The Ratio Dilemma

If you've made a restaurant style curry of twice the recipe portion sizes or more, you may have noticed it has a stronger taste. The effect of scaling up all the ingredients uniformly (i.e. in exact multiples of the original recipe) doesn't really work. The disproportionate effect that some ingredients (mainly spices) have on the curry becomes more noticeable the more you scale the recipe up. In other words, spices don't scale up in a straight line.

An Example

Let's say someone (who we will call Bob simply for brevity) decides to cook his family a nice chicken Madras for supper. Bob's got a family of four plus an invited neighbour to feed, and to make things easier he decides to cook four recipe portions in one go in a sizeable wok, which should be enough to feed everyone with a little left over.

Putting aside the 'heat' considerations (see previous section) for now, Bob calculates and weighs out x4 the amount of each ingredient. With all the prep done, first it's in with the oil, the whole seeds (cumin seeds and cassia bark in my Volume 1 recipe), the ginger/garlic paste, methi, and then the powdered spices (mix powder, chilli powder), tomato paste, chicken, and so on.

Feeling rather pleased with himself, Bob serves up the delicious-looking and seemingly perfectly cooked Madras to the small but eager crowd sitting patiently around the dining table. Comments of approval are muttered briefly while they are enjoying the presentation and aroma.

After encouragement from Bob to tuck in, the neighbour (who we will call Tony) is first to sample some of the curry's sauce. He loves a Madras curry and regularly devours one from the local takeaway without much fuss – the heat level is about right for him. Alarm bells start ringing in Tony's head. A disturbingly hot, harsh and bitter flavour assaults the front of his mouth, and when he swallows the pain spreads to the back of his throat. Tony's head feels like it's going to explode, and for a moment he loses all composure, but out of politeness he keeps his discomfort to himself.

Next to try the curry is Bob's wife, Emma. She also loves hot curry, but her face quickly turns a shade of red, and she gives Bob a stern stare across the table. Bob and his two children (Sam and Zoe) then tuck in. As well as the burning sensation, a sudden feeling of disappointment and shame engulf Bob, for he is an alpha male. His much (self)-acclaimed curry making has already made him a legend in his own kitchen (well at least since the previous Saturday when he cooked his first ever curry, a single recipe portion prawn bhuna). Oh Bob, hero to zero in five mouthfuls!

That imaginary situation may well be familiar to some people reading this. If you've persevered and experimented, you will no doubt have discovered that you need to adjust the scaled-up spices back down somewhat to prevent a culinary calamity.

Thankfully, all was not lost. Bob soon recognised the problem, and being a determined sort of bloke he persevered over the following weeks and cooked up delicious, sensible curries to the delight of his family, and indeed the whole street of neighbours (including Tony). But when Bob had the time, to get the best flavour possible he preferred to cook BIR curries for the masses by making multiple single recipe-sized portions.

The Compromise

When upscaling, to get the optimal flavour (and by that, I mean 'the best under the circumstances') adjustments are needed to both the ingredient ratios (the 'what'), and the method of cooking ('the how').

Spices and masalas are the main criminals that disobey the ratio rules, and the most blatant offender of those is chilli powder, closely followed by garam masala, coriander, cumin, cassia, and then pretty much any pungent spice. Powdered spices are more potent than when using the unground, whole version for infusing flavour.

With the BIR recipes in my books it's the spices in the previous paragraph that are used the most. However, some recipes may call for less frequently used but similarly potent spices such as tandoori masala, amchoor, cinnamon powder, chaat masala, and so on.

It's not just the spices that can cause problems. Salt should be scaled back, as should kasuri methi (dried fenugreek leaves) and acidic liquids such as lemon juice and vinegar. Also, I've found that different ingredients scale up in varying ratios. For example, kasuri methi is more forgiving than chilli powder.

Upscaling Cooking Method

Following on from the earlier 'Heat Dilemma' section, the most important adjustment when scaling up is attaining and maintaining the right level of heat to caramelise the sauce as best as possible.

To that end it's essential to add relatively small amounts of base gravy at a time in the early stages of cooking. In those early stages the base gravy can reach a higher temperature than later, when there will be a greater volume of ingredients in the pan. The higher temperature produces caramelisation for that all-important flavour. By reducing down small amounts of the base gravy at a time and then repeating the process, lots of flavour gets locked in.

While the upscaling cooking technique is closely aligned to that of single recipe portions, there are a couple of important distinctions.

Firstly, more time will be needed when cooking an upscaled BIR curry. There is more base gravy to cook, and with the limited heat/temperature it will obviously take longer to reduce. For example, while a single recipe portion curry may take 7-10 minutes, it may take up to 45-50 minutes to cook a x8 version. This distinction varies in magnitude dependent on the upscaling factor - obviously a x2 curry will take a lot less time than a x16 curry.

You may be wondering if a shortcut can be taken in using base gravy in its undiluted, thick state. In my opinion it's always best to use thin base gravy (with the consistency of semi-skimmed milk). The reason is that it gives the curry time to develop flavour when reducing down and produces a better texture. Curry cooked with thick base gravy tends to end up looking rather gloopy.

Secondly, a change is required to when the main ingredient is added. If the upscaled curry is going to take (say) 40 minutes to cook, you don't want to be adding in pre-cooked chicken, lamb or vegetables in the first few minutes as you would do for a single recipe portion BIR curry. It would not withstand the extended cooking period and would shred/mush as well as losing a lot of its flavour.

The same goes for raw chicken breast meat. It needs a longer time to cook, but only about 10-15 minutes, after which the chicken will start going rubbery. The raw chicken breast meat should therefore be added to the curry to give just enough time to cook/heat through properly so that it's as tender as possible.

With a suitably longer cooking time comes the opportunity to experiment with bone-in meat. Whilst it's not typical of the boneless pre-cooked meat and poultry normally used in British Indian Restaurants and takeaways, the bone adds a great flavour to a curry.

Red meats (raw) such as lamb, mutton, beef, etc., need an extended cooking time on a lowish heat. The 1½ hours or more required to get tender meat is clearly longer than it would take to cook the sauce in an upscaled BIR curry, so a further adjustment is needed.

For example, we normally cook a x4 recipe portion curry with pre-cooked chicken that would take (say) 35 minutes to make, but instead we want to make a version with raw, cubed on-the-bone leg of lamb. The lamb needs (say) 1½ hours to cook properly, which is a lot more than the 30 minutes or so it would take for the sauce to be ready (reduced down to the right consistency).

The way to do this is to add the lamb cubes near the beginning of cooking when the tomato paste is added. When the base gravy has been reduced enough, cover the pan and turn the heat down to low. (Covering the pan stops most of the steam from escaping and helps keep the sauce from becoming too thick.) Leave to cook for an hour, stir once or twice, and adjust the thickness with a bit of base gravy or water if required.

Cooking Vessels

Obviously it's a different ball game to make a cauldron full of curry to feed a small army than it is to cook enough to feed a small family. The size of the cooking vessel (frying pan, wok, korai, stockpot, etc.) should be appropriate to the amount of the ingredients. Other considerations include what the curry is being cooked on (hob, camping stove, high output gas burner, bonfire, etc.), and what material the cooking vessel is made of (aluminium, steel, non-stick, etc.).

Over on the right is a table in which I make some suggestions on what type and size of cooking vessel to use for a range of portion multiples for any given BIR style curry. The word 'aluminium' refers to the bare metal type of pan, as opposed to one with a non-stick coating.

Recipe Portions	Feeds (Adults)	Suggested Cooking Vessel (inner diameter rim to rim, capacity)	Notes
1+	2 (barely)	Aluminium frying pan (24-26cm)	Cooking method as per single recipe portion, but a bit more of the main ingredient and base gravy.
2	2-3	Aluminium frying pan (26-28cm)	
3	3-4	Large steel wok or korai	
4	4-6	Large aluminium saucepan or stockpot (24-28cm, 7 litres)	
6	6-9	Large aluminium saucepan or stockpot (28-30cm, 7-10 litres)	
8	9-12	Large aluminium saucepan or stockpot (30-32cm, 10-14 litres)	
16	20-24	Very large aluminium stockpot (36cm-40cm, 18-22 litres)	Straddle the pot over the hob to give the most heat coverage from the gas/electric rings.

Scaling Up Template

So, how about some useful practical numbers that can be used to scale up recipe ingredients? My experience in bulk catering led to me creating a spreadsheet of scaling factors. Here I have reproduced it for one of the most popular curries (chicken Madras), though it can of course be adapted for many types of BIR curry. It's based on the single portion recipe for chicken Madras in Volume 1.

You will find that spreadsheet on the opposite page, and please note that it's based on my opinions and practical experiences. I do not profess it to be a complete solution for every upscaling scenario. There are so many factors in play that it's practically impossible to articulate every possible combination of ingredients and ratios – cooking is not an exact science.

- The 'Scale Factor' percentages suggest how the quantity of any ingredient should be multiplied for each recipe portion size. For example, a x4 recipe portion Madras uses 1½ tsp of cumin seeds, which is three times what the single recipe portion states. In simpler (and probably more sensible) words, the cumin seeds have been toned down in proportion.
- The lighter shaded rows (also denoted with an asterisk after the ingredient name) depict those ingredients which scale up uniformly ('in a straight line').
- As with all recipes in this book, spoon measures are level unless stated otherwise. 1 tsp=5ml, and 1 TBSP=15ml.
- The suggested size of pot for the larger scaling factors may seem excessive, but the high sides help reduce the amount of curry sauce plopping and splattering everywhere.

Copyright © 2019 Richard Sayce

SCALING UP CHICKEN MADRAS

Ingredient	Unit	Single Recipe Portion (1 person) Quantity	x2 Recipe Portions (2-3 people) Qty	x2 Scale Factor	x3 Recipe Portions (3-4 people) Qty	x3 Scale Factor	x4 Recipe Portions (4-6 people) Qty	x4 Scale Factor	x6 Recipe Portions (6-9 people) Qty	x6 Scale Factor	x8 Recipe Portions (9-12 people) Qty	x8 Scale Factor	x16 Recipe Portions (20-24 people) Qty	x16 Scale Factor
Oil/Ghee	ml	60	100	1.67	145	2.42	180	3	260	4.33	330	5.5	625	10.42
Cassia Bark	cm	10	15	1.5	20	2	22	2.2	33	3.3	30	3	40	4
Cumin Seeds	tsp	0.5	1	2	1.25	2.5	1.5	3	2	4	2	5	3.5	7
Ginger/Garlic Paste *	tsp	2	4	2	6	3	8	4	12	6	16	8	32	16
Mix Powder	tsp	1.5	2.5	1.67	3.5	2.33	4.25	2.84	6	4	7.5	5	12	8
Chilli Powder	tsp	1.5	2.25	1.5	3	2	3.50	2.34	5	3.33	6	4	10	6.67
Salt	tsp	0.4	0.75	1.88	1	2.5	1.25	3.12	1.75	4.37	2	5	3.2	8
Kasuri Methi	tsp	1	1.75	1.75	2.5	2.5	3	3	4	4	5	5	8.5	8.5
Tomato Paste *	TBSP	5	10	2	15	3	20	4	30	6	40	8	80	16
Coriander Stalks *	TBSP	1	2	2	3	3	4	4	6	6	8	8	16	16
Base Gravy (diluted) *	ml	350	700	2	1050	3	1400	4	2100	6	2800	8	5600	16
Lemon Dressing/Juice	tsp	2	3.5	1.75	5	2.5	6	3	8.5	4.25	10.5	5.25	16	8
Worc. Sauce *	tsp	0.5	1	2	1.5	3	2	4	3	6	4	8	8	16
Pre-Cooked Chicken *	g	200	400	2	600	3	800	4	1200	6	1600	8	3200	16
Coriander Leaves *	TBSP	1	2	2	3	3	4	4	6	6	8	8	16	16
Suggested Cooking Vessel		Small frying pan	Large frying pan		Large kadai/wok or medium/large pan 5 litre capacity		Large pan 7 litre capacity		Large pan 7-10 litre capacity		Very large pan 10-14 litre capacity		Huge stockpot minimum 18 litre capacity	

Upscaling Curry 141

The template on the previous page is tailored specifically for the ingredients of a chicken Madras curry, so it doesn't show the upscaling factors for the many other ingredients used in other recipes.

The following table segregates the common BIR recipe ingredients into different bands. For each of these bands there is an array of numbers representing the suggested upscaling factor for the different recipe portion factors.

SCALING FACTOR BANDS	INGREDIENTS	SUGGESTED INGREDIENT UPSCALE FACTOR					
		x2	x3	x4	x6	x8	x16
Band A	Oil, Ghee	1¾	2½	3	4½	5½	10½
Band B	Base Gravy, Poultry/Meat/Seafood/Vegetables/Fruit, Ginger/Garlic Paste, Tomato Paste, Onion, Fresh Coriander, Coconut Milk, Coconut Powder, Ground Almond, Sugar, Honey, Jaggery etc.	2	3	4	6	8	16
Band C	Spice Seeds - e.g. Fennel, Cumin, Black Mustard	2	2½	3	4	5	7
Band D	Salt, Chaat Masala, Kasuri Methi, Lemon or Lime Juice, Amchoor powder	1¾	2½	3	4	5	8½
Band E	Mix Powder, Cumin Powder, Tandoori Masala, Curry Powder, Turmeric, Elachi Powder etc.	1½ - 1¾	2¼	2¾	4	5	8
Band F	Whole spices excluding seeds - e.g. Cassia Bark, Star Anise, Bay Leaf, Clove etc.	1½	2	2¼	3¼	3	4
Band G	Chilli Powder (all types)	1½	2	2¼	3¼	4	6¾

Let's see how this works by picking out one ingredient to upscale.

For example, you want to cook a x3 recipe portion of curry that features tandoori masala. The single portion version requires 2 tsp of tandoori masala, so to work out how much is needed for a x3 recipe portion, the first thing to do is identify which 'band' tandoori masala sits in (band 'E').

You then find the number where the table row intersects with the x3 column. In this case it's 2¼, which is the number you use to multiply the original single portion ingredient amount by for the 3 portions.

So, 2 tsp of tandoori masala multiplied by 2¼ gives a total of 4½ tsp of tandoori masala for a x3 recipe portion.

Got that? Phew!

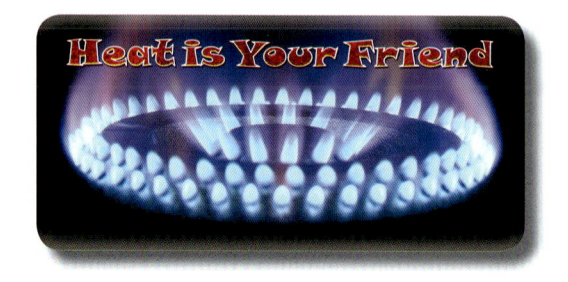

142 Upscaling Curry

Example: Chicken Madras for 4-6

Here's a detailed recipe for making a x4 recipe portion of BIR Madras curry in one pan, using the data in the above scaling tables. I'm using pre-cooked chicken in this recipe, but any main ingredient can be added to it, for example chicken tikka or pre-cooked lamb.

Arguably the most crucial part of the cooking method in the recipe is the repeated addition of small amounts of base gravy near the beginning of cooking. The temperature in the pan is highest when there's not much volume in the pan, so that's the best time to utilise the heat to caramelise the sauce to release excellent flavour.

I recommend using a stockpot or saucepan of at least 7 litres capacity, and preferably made of aluminium without a non-stick coating. Aluminium pans distribute heat well, and the curry sauce will stick to the surface and caramelise nicely.

A steel saucepan can be used instead, but there is a greater risk that the sauce will burn because of the 'hot-spots' of uneven heat distribution. Conversely, non-stick cookware will remove the concern of burning a curry, but it will not caramelise the sauce as well as pans with aluminium or steel surfaces.

The curry will bubble and splatter a lot while cooking, which is why a large capacity cooking vessel is recommended. I would avoid using a large wok or korai for a recipe of this proportion simply because of all the oily curry splatters that would coat you and your kitchen environment.

Feeds four to six people, depending on appetite. There's a YouTube video for this recipe showing how it's made. Scan the QR Code at the top-right of this page to watch it.

Upscaling Curry

Ingredients

- 180ml Oil
- 20cm Cassia Bark
- 1½ tsp Cumin Seeds
- 2½ TBSP Ginger/Garlic Paste
- 4¼ tsp Mix Powder
- 3½ tsp Chilli Powder
- 1¼ tsp Salt
- 3 tsp Kasuri Methi
- 20 TBSP Tomato Paste (300ml). See Notes
- 4 TBSP Coriander Stalks, finely chopped
- 1.4 litres Base Gravy (diluted and heated up)
- 6 tsp Lemon Juice
- 2 tsp Worcestershire Sauce
- 800-1000g of the main ingredient (Pre-cooked or Raw Chicken, Lamb, etc.). See Notes
- 4 TBSP Coriander Leaves, finely chopped

Method

1. Add the oil to the pan/stockpot on medium high heat.
2. Add the cassia bark and cumin seeds when the oil has heated up and fry for 30-45 seconds, stirring once or twice.
3. Then add the ginger/garlic paste and fry for another 30-45 secs, stirring diligently to prevent it burning.
4. Now add the mix powder, chilli powder, kasuri methi, and salt. Mix together, then after 5-10 seconds stir in 100ml base gravy (hot). Leave it to fry for 30 seconds.
5. Turn the heat up to high and add the tomato paste and coriander stalks. Stir together and leave alone to fry for 2 minutes.
6. Add a second 100ml of base gravy, scrape the bottom and sides of the pan to mix everything, then leave for 1½ minutes.
7. Repeat the previous stage a further two times, so that a total 400ml of base gravy has been added so far. Adding the base gravy a little at a time in several stages is crucial for getting the best flavour – it helps keep the temperature high and for caramelisation to happen while there's still not much volume in the pan. As the recipe progresses more is put in, which hinders the all-important temperature needed for getting the best flavour.
8. Now stir in 400ml of base gravy and scrape any caramelised residue from the bottom and sides of the pan back into the sauce.
9. Cover the pan and leave the sauce to cook for 5 minutes. This will raise the temperature and help the sauce to caramelise at the bottom of the pan.
10. Next add 600ml base gravy, the lemon juice and the Worcestershire sauce.
11. Scrape and stir the pan, then let cook for 15 minutes, uncovered. Stir it no more than once or twice in that time period.
12. Finally, add the main ingredient and mix it well into the sauce.
13. If the main ingredient you are using is pre-cooked (e.g. chicken, chicken tikka, pre-cooked lamb, prawns), then you just need to cook it for a further 5 minutes, keeping the heat on high.
14. However, raw meat will need a longer cooking time, and with the heat reduced so that it can be safely left to cook without burning. Use the following timings as a guide and see the Notes section for further information.
    - Boneless chicken breast: 10-15 minutes, low-medium heat
    - Boneless chicken thigh: 15 mins, low-medium heat

- Bone-in chicken thigh, breast, leg: 30 mins, low heat, gentle simmer

15. You will notice a lot of oil floating on the surface, most of which can be scooped out with a ladle or large spoon. Don't throw it away though – this 'seasoned' oil has a superb flavour and is excellent to start cooking other curries with.

16. Just before the end of cooking stir in the fresh coriander leaves, and it's ready.

Notes

a) Bear in mind that raw chicken will release liquid when cooking, which will thin the sauce down somewhat.

b) Prepare the tomato paste by mixing 5 TBSP of double concentrated tomato purée with 15 TBSP (225ml) of water. Alternatively use ¾ of a tin of plum tomatoes, blended to a paste.

c) Also consider that cooked chicken will weigh approximately 20% less than raw, so adjust the amount you use upwards accordingly. In my opinion a decent curry portion size contains 200g of cooked chicken, which is easily enough to satisfy a hungry adult.

Imaginary Upscaling Scenarios

OK, so a x4 chicken Madras recipe curry is one thing, but what about other circumstances? Let's look at some fictitious scenarios of how BIR style curry recipes might be upscaled in various amounts. Naturally, these examples are for 'one pot' cooking and exclude situations when several different curries are being cooked as individual recipe portions served for the same meal.

1 Recipe Portion + a bit more

A cosy lamb jalfrezi for two people made by cooking the single recipe portion in a frying pan, but adding a little bit of extra base gravy and some more of the main ingredient (i.e. pre-cooked lamb). It's just enough to feed the couple along with their chosen accompaniments of rice and onion bhaji.

2 Recipe Portions

This time it's a small family affair. Mum, dad, and their young son sit down to eat a chicken jalfrezi, which was cooked in a medium-large wok. The ingredients were double except for wisely toning down the spices a little, and the method was followed exactly. The jalfrezi took a bit longer to cook because there was double the volume in the frying pan.

Accompanied by naan and an onion salad, the family was amply fed. The curry tasted good, but mum commented that it wasn't quite as good as the previous time when dad had cooked a single recipe portion just for her. The jalfrezi lacked some of the 'vibrance' associated with high cooking temperatures.

4 Recipe Portions

It's a small dinner party of five hungry adults gathered for a curry night. Keema dopiaza has been cooked in a 7-litre non-stick saucepan and is plated up alongside some plain basmati rice. There's enough for everybody, just.

This was the first time Jim (the host and cook) had tried upscaling a recipe. He had a copy of this book to hand, so he referred to the scaling up template earlier in the book for guidance on how to scale up the ingredients, and to the method section of the x4 upscaled Madras recipe for the general technique. Jim's usual implement for cooking BIR style curry is his treasured bare aluminium 26cm frying pan, but the only pan he has big enough for the upscaled curry is his 7-litre non-stick saucepan.

While cooking the dopiaza, Jim makes a few observations. Firstly, and unsurprisingly, the sauce does not cling to the pan while thickening like it does when he uses a bare aluminium pan. He reconciles this when he later tastes it, finding the flavour good but lacking a certain 'oomph'.

Secondly, the curry takes longer than he expected it to finish – over 30 minutes in total. With a larger volume of ingredients being added to the pan the average temperature has dropped, despite the gas flame on his hob being on its highest setting. This means the base gravy takes significantly longer to reduce down to the right thickness.

Thirdly, Jim is alarmed at the amount of bubbling, plopping and volcano-like splattering, especially in the last half of the cooking time. He had initially thought the pan was too big for the job, but ends up pleased that the sides of the pan are quite deep. Using a shallower pan would have meant even more messy splutters.

6 Recipe Portions

The sun is shining, and Val has invited nine of her friends over to enjoy curry and drinks in the garden. In preparation she upscales a chicken tikka pathia recipe by a factor of six, and decides on an 8-litre aluminium stockpot to cook it in. There's hardly a breath of wind, so Val decides to cook the curry outside on a powerful gas burner. Like Jim, she has a copy of this book and takes on board the suggestions for ingredient ratios and adjusted cooking method.

A fantastic aroma permeates the neighbourhood while she cooks the pathia. Val notices how well the sauce is caramelising in the early stages when she's added only a little at a time, and that the capable flame of the gas burner is helping to keep the temperature high as more and more of the base gravy is added. She's glad she didn't use a cheap camping stove – its low heat output simply wouldn't cut the mustard. There's one thing Val would do differently next time, and that's to wear an apron. The curry splattered everywhere! A bigger pot with higher sides would also be a good idea for that quantity of curry.

Anyhow, the guests enjoyed the chicken tikka pathia. So much so there was a brief argument over who would get to take the small amount of leftovers home with them! Val's garden parties became legendary, in no small part because of her using the most suitable curry cooking equipment and techniques. The garden patio has become a permanent yellow and orange impressionist work of art.

8 Recipe Portions

Luke is ambitious but headstrong. Although he's not really cooked Indian food before, he regularly makes roast Sunday dinner with all the trimmings to feed his large, extended, and noisy family, so he's comfortable with cooking for a crowd. But this Sunday is different – Luke wants to serve a curry with accompaniments to the 11 family members who invade the house every weekend.

He's found a (single portion) BIR style recipe for lamb rogan josh on YouTube that he likes the look of, so without further thought or ado, Luke multiplies all the ingredients by eight, which he knows should be enough for all 12 of them.

Having pre-cooked the lamb and prepared the base gravy, he then digs out his epic and posh stainless steel 15 litre pot that his wife gave him last Christmas. Glad to have found a worthy use for it, he heaves it on top of his induction hob.

Thus, early on Sunday morning he launches eagerly into making the rogan josh, referring to the notes he scribbled down from the YouTube video and his upscaled ingredient assumption, which is to multiply every ingredient by eight!

From the time he adds the ginger/garlic paste, things start getting hectic. The induction hob is very fast and efficient, and Luke has to continually stir to stop the paste burning. Steel has quite uneven heat distribution and 'hotspots' exist on the surface where the temperature gets hotter than other areas. This can lead to the pan contents sticking and burning more easily than pans made of aluminium, so more stirring is needed.

Undeterred, Luke quickly continues with the recipe, adjusts his approach, and diligently stirs to avoid burning. He does, however, correctly follow what the captions mentioned in the recipe video – to let the sauce stick and caramelise.

Finally, after much wrist action, huffing and puffing and plopping and splattering, he decides the lamb rogan josh is ready. Once he's spooned off most of the floating oil, Luke grabs a teaspoon and tastes a sample. Disaster! The curry is over-spiced and over-salted to such an extent that it's unsalvageable. He's just learned painfully that scaling up is not as simple as he thought.

The local carvery pub becomes the venue for that day's Sunday lunch, where Luke drowns his sorrows. He shouldn't be despondent because the only thing he did wrong was to multiply the ingredients incorrectly, and, after all, he wasn't to know. On subsequent Sundays he experiments, and through trial and error gets the right balance of spicing that makes everyone happy.

16 Recipe Portions

Remember Bob from earlier? Well, word has spread about his curry cooking and the local community centre has asked him if he'd like to set up an Indian food stall at the annual Spring Fair to cater for the attendees.

Relishing the challenge, Bob decides to make (among other things) a batch of chicken pasanda curry big enough to serve about 24 lunchtime diners. It just so happens that Bob has recently invested in an excellent curry cookbook that has a dedicated chapter on upscaling. Within it he finds guidelines on the ingredient ratios, and he reads all the advice given. He opts to cook one very big pot of pasanda following the book's recipe and suggestion for x16 ingredient ratios, which he estimates will be enough fayre for the fair (pardon the pun) to feed the 24 or so.

With the perfect excuse to visit his favourite Asian supermarket, Bob returns from his shopping pilgrimage with a very large aluminium cooking pot (44cm diameter, 18cm height, 22½ litre capacity). Just right for the job.

Bob gets up very early on the day of the fair to make the curry. He's already made the base gravy and pre-cooked the chicken the day before, so he's pretty much ready to go. Such a big pan has a large surface area, and when on the kitchen gas hob it can straddle the lion's share of the gas rings. "That's convenient", Bob ponders. "I need all the heat I can get to cook this bad boy!"

So, he turns all four gas rings on, and to cut a long recipe short, using his experience and the guidance from his coveted book he cooks a delicious chicken pasanda, sets up stall at the fair, and sells it all in half an hour.

That evening, after a tiring day, Bob is at home relaxing on the sofa with a pint of Cobra lager, feeling pleased with himself. He's got a right to feel a bit smug; after all he used all the skills he's picked up along the way, both from the curry cookbook and his own experimentations.

Bob picks up the well-thumbed book and once again reads the chapter about scaling up curry. He ponders the paradox.

Pumping Up the Temperature

High output gas burners are excellent at replicating the equipment used in Indian restaurant kitchens, and those that I have used range in power from about 7 kWh to 10 kWh.

For safety reasons these need to be used outside or in a suitably ventilated and safeguarded enclosed area such as a shed. When used outdoors they are restricted by any breeze or ambient temperature and it's advisable to use a good wind shield to avoid heat loss. Obviously high output burners require a gas supply (usually a gas cylinder) and the appropriate connection equipment (regulator and hose).

In the ideal circumstances a high output burner can help make superb tasting double recipe size portions. However, even with the extra power over a domestic hob, if you scale up further, for example three to four times, the results won't be as good. Having said that every little extra bit of power is a good thing.

Summary

- As ever with BIR cooking, heat and temperature are your friends. Use as high a heat source as you can (without burning any ingredients of course) and make the most of it. The average temperature in the pan/pot will drop as more and more ingredients are added, especially voluminous ones such as base gravy (even when it's poured in hot). Don't waste heat by stirring unnecessarily.

- Don't be tempted to add larger quantities of base gravy at a time until you've caramelised at least three or more of the initial small amounts. For larger recipe scale factors repeat the process even more. For example, in the x4 chicken Madras recipe above, the base gravy is added initially in four 100ml batches. I would suggest increasing the number of these 'batches' further for even larger portion curries, while keeping the volume of liquid in each batch small.

- Some ingredients (especially spices) will overpower the taste of a curry if scaled up exactly by the number of recipe portions being cooked at a time. Use the suggested upscaling factors detailed earlier in this chapter as a basis.

- The main ingredient of a scaled up curry is better added towards the end of cooking (dependent on the overall cooking time) so that it doesn't overcook.

- Use a high-sided cooking pot/pan. As you will most probably have experienced with single recipe portion curry cooking, there is often a lot of mess from curry sauce splattering out of the frying pan. The mess is even greater when cooking larger curry portion sizes, and a high-sided pot helps to contain the spluttering.

- Don't expect your upscaled curry to taste quite as good (on average) as one cooked as a single recipe portion. If you have time to do so, cook each recipe portion individually.

Inside an Indian Restaurant Kitchen

INTRODUCTION

Well, yes, this book is all about making restaurant style food at home, but it would seem remiss not to have a peek inside a professional kitchen. As I'm sure you can imagine, there's a great deal of difference between the way a professional chef operates and how we cook at home.

In this chapter I'll make some observations about working life in the kitchens of British Indian Restaurants and takeaways, accompanied with some photos taken during my visits. Herein I'll use the word 'chef' to refer collectively to the head chef and all the kitchen staff who work under him or her, whether they be sous chefs, tandoori chefs, or the hard-working kitchen porter who does the washing up.

The photographs in this chapter were all taken during a couple of visits to Bindi of Aspull, an excellent Indian restaurant under new management (2018) near Wigan, Lancashire. The owners generously allowed me access to the kitchen to spend time with the kitchen staff and record footage during a relatively quiet period of service.

Although most of the mainstream British Indian Restaurants have Bangladeshi chefs, Bindi of Aspull has a Nepalese head chef called Santosh, who is also a co-owner. Santosh, who has many years' experience in South Asian catering internationally, adopted the mainstream BIR method of cooking as part of his role when he joined Bindi.

The restaurant's menu consists mostly of your typical BIR fare (classic curries, signature dishes, tandoori grills, etc.), as that's what the local clientele has become accustomed to over the years and come in droves to eat. However, the head chef subsequently introduced some Nepalese-inspired specials, such as momos, vegetable manchurian, and spicy lamb kidney. Having sampled those amazing delights I'm confident they will become firm favourites with the regular customers.

I've been lucky enough to spend time in a fair few restaurant kitchens, and each differs in its methods of preparation and cooking. The chefs I've spoken with pride themselves in their own touches to make their curries that bit unique and special, and each has their own way of preparing base gravies and all the other pre-cooked ingredients. It may sometimes seem that BIR cooking is quite narrow in scope, but I'm continually surprised at the variety of different ways of 'skinning a cat'.

For various reasons, kitchen staff turnover can be quite high. Also, no-one can be expected to work seven days a week on a long-term basis, so on any given day a customer is not guaranteed to be served food that's been cooked by the same chef as their previous visit.

This means an ongoing challenge of maintaining the quality and consistency of food. I'm sure many readers of this book at some point in their curry-eating career will have experienced the disappointment of a specific curry not tasting the same as on previous visits. It may have been a good curry, but perhaps you'd grown to love the usual taste?

One of the most likely causes is that the head chef is having a night off, and a sous chef fills the role for the evening. Although highly competent, he/she doesn't have quite the same level of experience as his/her senior colleague, nor the well-honed skill born out of intensive daily curry cooking.

Once I spoke to a chef who gave me his opinion on how curries can be different. He (Anwar) told me that you can demonstrate the same recipe to two different chefs and ask each of them to cook it. He concluded that the two curries would not taste identical because of very small variables in individual cooking techniques and tendencies. A few examples of this are slight variations in the measurement of ingredients, the cooking time and order, and the level of heat applied.

PREPARATION & SPEED

The primary challenge that a chef faces is to satisfy customers by fulfilling their orders within a reasonable time, and to a good, consistent standard. This is dependent on several things that need to be in place to keep the cogs oiled, axles greased, and the wheels spinning.

BIR food is cooked to order quickly – it simply has to be. Most if not all curries on the menu are impractical to prepare well in advance of customers ordering. It would take far too long and there would be huge amounts of wasted food.

Figure A: Kitchen Overview. Top left and bottom left: lengthwise view from two opposite directions. Top right: view of kitchen from doorway, service station front left of photo. Bottom right: chefs at work.

Each curry is cooked to order, so all the component parts must be instantly available to the chef. I used 'cooked' in the previous sentence, but perhaps a better word is 'assembled'. Most of the ingredients (e.g. chicken, lamb, base gravy, service onions) have been pre-cooked in advance, and the curry is (in very simplistic terms) being thrown together in a frying pan and finished off on high heat for five minutes or so.

That is why preparation is so important in commercial BIR kitchens. For instance, it would be unfortunate and somewhat disastrous if the pre-cooked chicken or lamb ran out half-way through service on a busy Saturday evening.

Aside from the curries (and other menu items that are pan-fried), starters and accompaniments also use ingredients that have been prepared earlier. Rice is probably the best example. During service, takeaways and restaurants always have a supply of ready-made pilau and plain rice to hand, often cooked in very large batches to last a day or more.

Naan and other breads are also prepared in advance. It only takes a few minutes to cook a naan in a tandoor oven, but the dough needs preparing earlier to give it time to rest and prove. To quickly bake a naan, the tandoori chef grabs a proven ball of dough from the many he/she prepared earlier, rolls it out on the worktop, then slaps it into the tandoor oven.

Figure B: Curry Station. Left: head chef Santosh cooking chicken tikka masala. Top middle: pre-cooked chicken, service onions, and other prepared ingredients. Top right: worktop and shelving for additional handy ingredients. Bottom right: array of gas burners sporting the all-essential pot of base gravy, with a rack of spice-filled gastronorms and frying pans above.

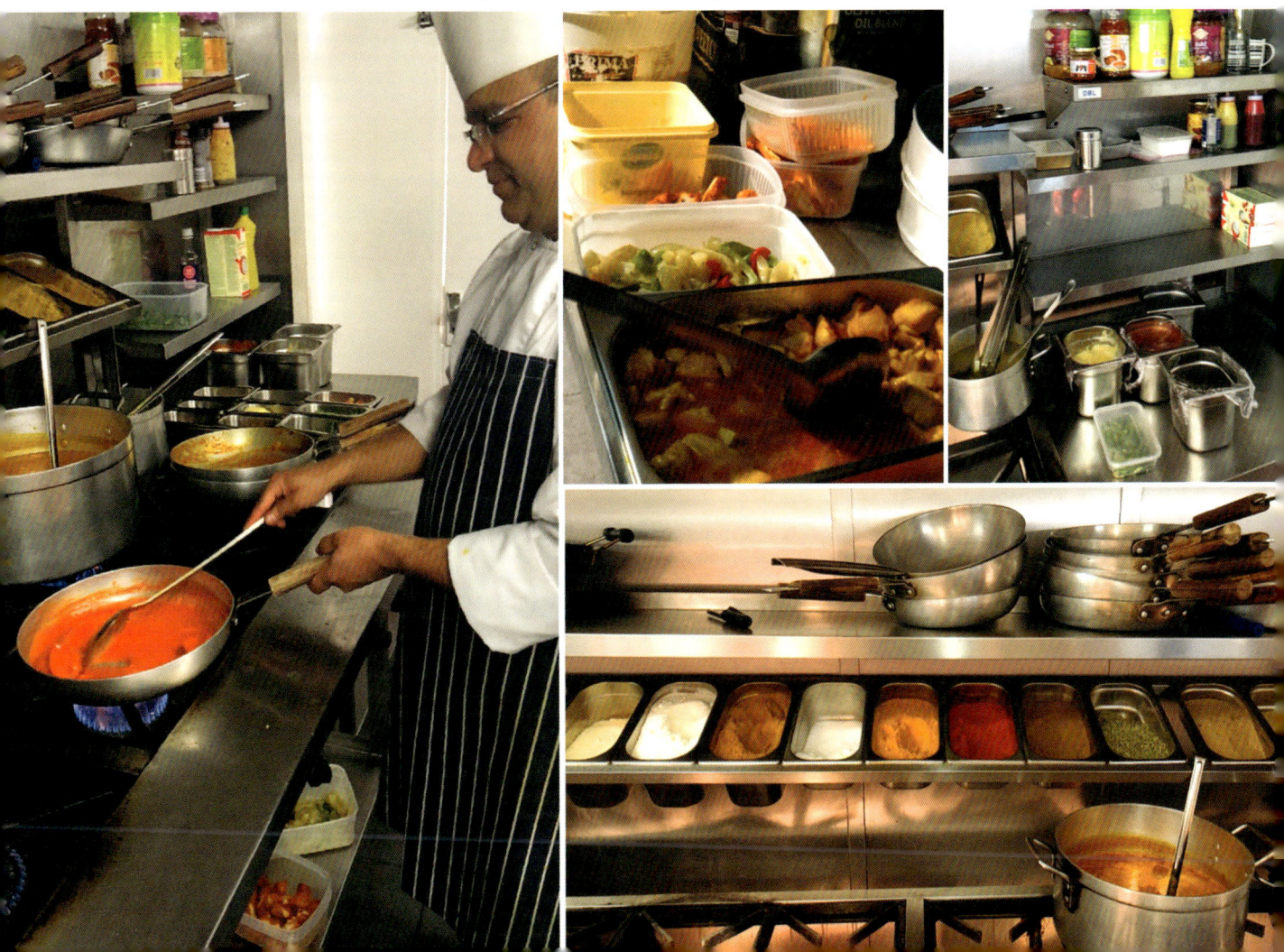

Onion bhajis may only take around five minutes to fry from their raw state, but that time is not quite short enough to fulfil demand for this highly popular item when the kitchen is inundated with orders. The onion bhajis can be par-cooked in advance of serving, and then refried briefly when needed.

Every time-saving measure makes the process a little smoother. Some curries (e.g. jalfrezi, balti) include chunks of onion and pepper, which take far too long to cook from raw, so BIR kitchens usually fry or poach them in advance. The same can also said to a lesser extent about 'service onions', those finely chopped onions used in a multitude of dishes. Although the small size of the raw onion pieces means they will cook quickly, I've seen some restaurant kitchens prepare a tub full of pre-fried service onions simply to shave a little time from the final curry 'end game'.

So, in a nutshell, preparation is paramount. A ready supply of all ingredients must be maintained. Nothing must run out if at all possible, and dwindling supplies should be anticipated and replenished accordingly.

Figure C: Prep Station. Top left: chopped chicken tikka. Bottom left: deep fat fryers. Middle: chopping onions. Top right: chicken chaat puri being assembled. Bottom right: Shahadath, sous chef.

QUALITY & COST

I'm sure that most readers will know that the catering business is a tough one. The long hours, hard work and very low profit margins are a constant challenge. There's little or no profit in selling a curry after all costs have been factored in (overheads, ingredients, staff costs, interest payments, insurance, gas and electricity, etc.).

A takeaway or restaurant would not survive if the only thing on the menu was curry (unless of course the main ingredient was a very cheap vegetable such as potato or cabbage). The profit margin is much greater on all the extra items that customers also order, such as poppadoms, rice, naan, onion bhajis, etc. Each of those example 'extras' has cheap ingredient costs, and so that little extra gross profit from each one helps keep the accountant happy (ah yes... the accountant... that's yet another cost). And Indian restaurants, of course, also benefit from the margin from alcohol and especially soft drinks.

As a sundry yet hugely popular menu item, the quintessential poppadom is the perfect example of a cash cow. They are bought very cheaply from wholesalers and large Asian supermarkets in tall plastic-wrapped stacks in their flat, uncooked state. Poppadoms take only a few seconds each to deep fry, and keep fresh for a surprisingly long time (at least 12 hours) if kept sealed in a warm, dry place, such as a commercial warming cupboard or very low oven. So, costing a few pence and sold to the customer at (say) 60p or more, you can understand why you're usually asked by the waiter if you want any poppadoms with your order, and why you might perceive the almost undetectable air of disappointment should you decline.

Figure D: Tandoori Station. Left: marinated chicken tikka baking in the tandoor oven. Top right: tandoor chef Raj preparing a naan, with tandoor oven in the background. Bottom right: a freshly cooked naan.

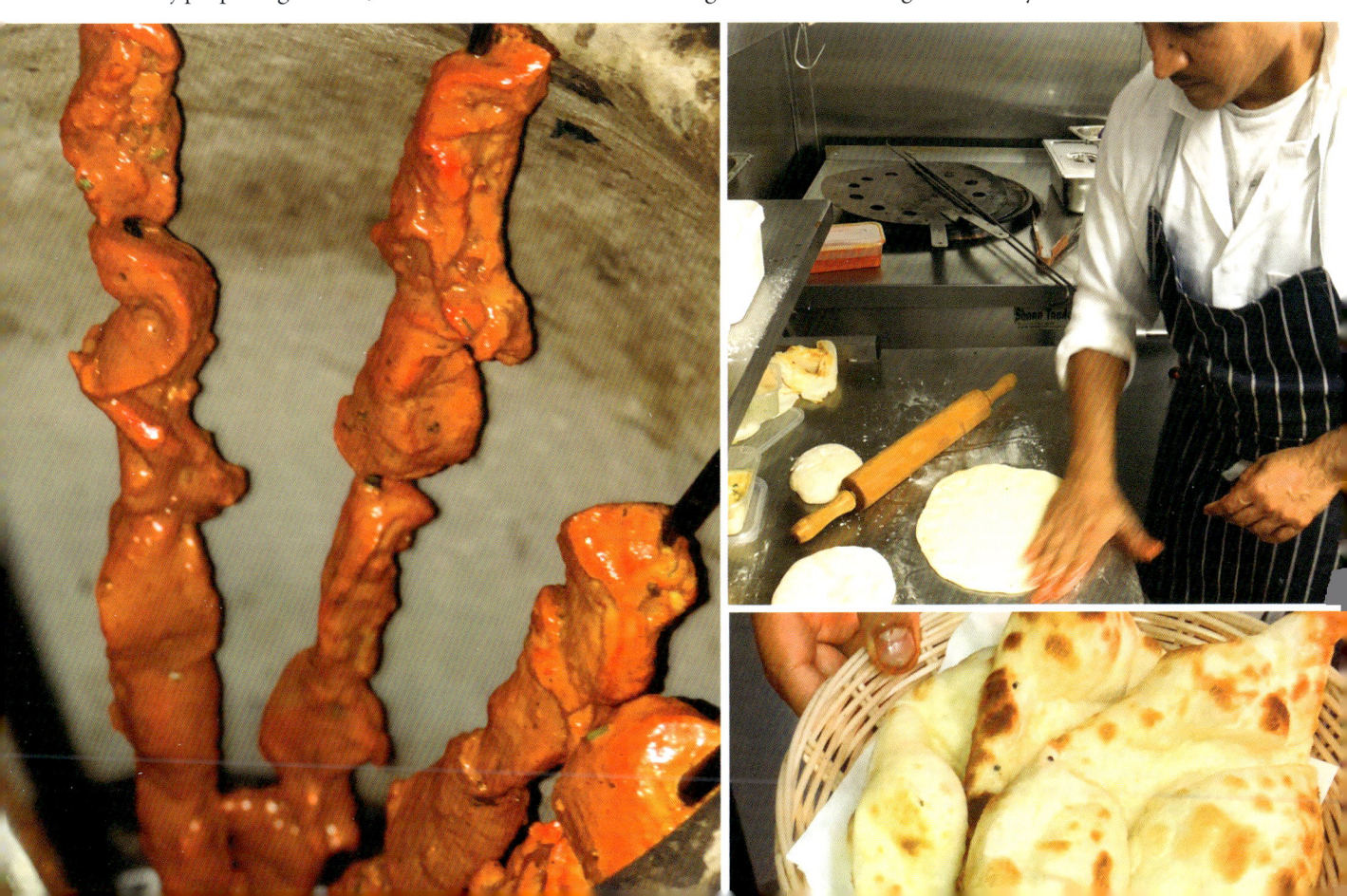

Figure E: Service Station. Left, from top to bottom: chicken tikka starter, stuffed pepper chicken chaat, chicken tikka masala, naan. Right: curries, rice and naan on the service counter awaiting collection by front of house staff.

There's no doubt that British Indian Restaurants and takeaways need to keep costs down. In addition to the running costs there's intense competition within the sector, so market forces mean the prices that customers are charged are held back.

Sadly, that all too often affects the quality of the food, and in recent years I'm one of many who have perceived a general deterioration. While some lament the passing of the 'good old days' when BIR food seemed to taste that bit better, I'm convinced part of that thinking is down to nostalgia. Nevertheless, that doesn't change the overall consensus, or the fact that over the last 7-10 years there has been an ever-increasing shortage of skilled chefs and other restaurant staff.

From a personal perspective, however, I can say that most meals from the Indian restaurants I've chosen to eat at in recent years have been excellent.

A SNEAKY PEEK

During visits to the kitchen at Bindi of Aspull, I managed to record some video footage of orders being cooked. It was a Sunday mid-afternoon and the restaurant had just opened for the day, a time that was relatively quiet (but got very busy later).

I've cobbled the footage together into three videos, which you can watch on YouTube by scanning the corresponding QR codes with a smart phone or other device. The second video is quite long and mostly unedited to give you a sense of timing, and it gives some very interesting insights into the way that this particular chef cooks curry. Please excuse the poor camerawork.

Video 1: Some starters, naan, and rice

Video 2: Curries (various)

Video 3: Time-lapse recording of 90 mins kitchen action

Figure F: Top left: head chef Santosh, tandoori chef Raj, sous chef Shahadath. Bottom left: part of the large dining area. Top right: exterior view, Bindi of Aspull. Bottom right: buffet area at menu relaunch event.

Chicken Madras (Volume 1) Chips with Curry - Tasty or Taboo ?

Acknowledgements

Special thanks (in no particular order) to Gary Crossley, Paul Clay, Anthony Green, Derek Price, Vonnie Braine, Lee Wiltshire, Anwar Hussain, Graham and Korina Taylor, Alex Wilkie, Nick Johnson (Carlton Print), Rob Somerville, Dion Heap, Andy Lees, Bob Flanagan, Richard Lupton, Graham Warburton, Amina Jane Ishaq, Rod Brown, Mark Horton and Shane Robinson.

Extra special thanks to Manoj and Bhavna Patel, Santosh, Maya, and everyone else at Bindi of Aspull - 2 Lucas Nook, Aspull, Wigan WN2 1PP (01942 833844).

There are so many other people I would like to acknowledge for their enthusiasm and support. The list is very long and seemingly unending, so I won't elaborate in case I miss anyone out, except to say many, many thanks to all.

Instead you'll find photos throughout the book showing off some of the food that the followers of Misty Ricardo's Curry Kitchen have submitted on Facebook. Perhaps you are one of them? If you spot a photo that you took let me know the page and position, and I'll send you a free poppadom!

Chicken Tikka Karahi (Volume 1)   Photo: Shaun Lindon

Index

A
Achari Chicken Tikka 26
Achari Lamb 48
Acknowledgements 157
Adrak 68
asafoetida 42

B
banana 62
Base Gravy 8, 16
    Base Gravy (Mark I) 6, 16
    Base Gravy (Mark II) 12
    Pressure Cooking Base Gravy 13
Bassar Mix Powder 11, 12
    Brands 11
Bhindi Fry 41
Black pepper 54
Brinjal Bhaji 37

C
Chaat masala 79
Chana Masala 100
Chicken Madras for 4-6 143
Chicken Pakoras 33
    Pakora Sauce 33
Chicken Tikka 6, 8, 21, 66
    Achari Chicken Tikka 26
    Chicken Tikka Shashlik 66
    Malai Chicken Tikka 28
Chicken Tikka Shashlik 66
Cooking Vessels 140
Coriander & Lemon Achari Mirch 44
Cumin & Onion Pilau 112

E
Egg Bhuna 92

F
Facebook 7
fenugreek 46
Follower's Photos 5, 14, 160
Freezing Ingredients 8

G
Getting Started 8
ginger 68
Ginger/Garlic Paste 6, 18
Gourmand World Cookbook Awards 4

H
Hing 42
Homestyle Lamb Curry 128

I
Indian Restaurant Kitchen 149
    A Sneaky Peek 155
    Introduction 149
    Preparation & Speed 150
    Quality & Cost 153
Instagram 7

K
Kadai Paneer 105
Kalimirch 54
Kashmir 61
Keema Peas 30

L
Lamb Chana Saagwala 73
LavaStorm 84
Lemon Rice 110

M
Malai Chicken Tikka 28
Mango Chicken 78
Methi Chicken 46
Misty Ricardo's Curry Kitchen 2, 4, 7, 85, 112, 157
Mix Powder
    Bassar Mix Powder 11
    Mix Powder (Volume 1) 6, 15
Moghul 64
Mr Naga 82
Mushroom Bhaji 39
mustard 71

N
New Mix Powder & Base Gravy 10

O
Okra 41

P
paneer 102, 106
Pasanda 80
Portion Sizes 6
Prawn Puri 24

Pre-Cooked Chicken 6, 8, 19
Pre-cooked Keema 30
Pre-Cooked Lamb 6, 8, 20
Pre-Prepared Ingredients 8, 15
    Base Gravy (Mark II) 12, 16
    Chicken Tikka (Volume 1) 6, 8, 21
    Ginger/Garlic Paste 6
    Lamb Stock 21
    Mix Powder (Volume 1) 15
    Pre-Cooked Chicken 6, 8, 19
    Pre-cooked Keema 30
    Pre-Cooked Lamb 6, 8, 20
    Tomato Paste 6, 18
Pudina 58
Punjabi Vegetable 'Staff' Curry 97

R

Recipe Conventions & Measurements 6
Restaurant Style Curries 43
    Achari Lamb 48
    Adrak 68
    Chicken Madras for 4-6 143
    Chicken Tikka Shashlik 66
    Coriander & Lemon Achari Mirch 44
    Kalimirch 54
    Kashmir 61
    King Prawn Zafrani 51
    Lamb Chana Saagwala 73
    LavaStorm 84
    Mango Chicken 78
    Methi Chicken 46
    Moghul 64
    Mr Naga 82
    Pasanda 80
    Pudina 58
    Shahee Chicken Tikka 75
    Shimla Mirch 56
    Shorshe Masala 70
    South Indian Tamarind 88
Rice 109
    Cumin & Onion Pilau 112
    Lemon Rice 110

S

Saag Paneer 102
Saffron 52, 53
Scaling Factor Ingredient Table 142
Scaling Up Curry. See Upscaling Curry
Shahee Chicken Tikka 75
Shimla Mirch 56
Shorshe Masala 70
South Indian Tamarind 88
Special Vegetarian Curries 91
spinach 73

Spinach & Mushroom Balti 94
Starters & Sides 23
    Achari Chicken Tikka 26
    Bhindi Fry 41
    Brinjal Bhaji 37
    Chicken Pakoras 33
    Keema Peas 30
    Malai Chicken Tikka 28
    Mushroom Bhaji 39
    Prawn Puri 24
    Vegetable Samosa 35
Street Food & Other Oddities 113
    Chutney, Chilli & Tomato 114

T

Tamarind 88
Tomato Paste 6, 18
    Blend tinned or fresh tomatoes 18
    Passata 18
    Tomato purée 18
Twitter 7

U

Upscaling Curry
    Chicken Madras for 4-6 143
    Cooking Vessels 140
    Scaling Factor Ingredient Table 142
    Scaling Up Template 140
    Upscaling Cooking Method 138
    Upscaling Scenarios 145
    Upscaling Summary 148

V

Vegetable Samosa 35
Vegetarian Curries 91
    Chana Masala 100
    Egg Bhuna 92
    Kadai Paneer 105
    Punjabi Vegetable 'Staff' Curry 97
    Saag Paneer 102
    Spinach & Mushroom Balti 94
Volume 1 4, 6, 7, 8, 9, 11, 15, 25, 31, 61, 74, 77, 81, 84, 85, 99, 101, 112, 136, 137, 140

Y

YouTube 7

Z

Zafrani 51

Photo Collage C: Just looking at this lot makes me hungry, especially the King Prawn Puri (1st column, 2nd row), by Vicky Forster.